THE
LITTLE FELLOW

The Little Fellow

The Life and Work of Charles Spencer Chaplin

by PETER COTES *and* THELMA NIKLAUS

with a Foreword by W. Somerset Maugham

THE CITADEL PRESS   NEW YORK

PN
2287
C5
C6
1965

Photographs reproduced through the courtesy of the British Film
Institute, Keystone Press Agency, Monidale Ltd., United Artists
Corporation, and the Museum of Modern Art (New York).

In memory of Sydney Bennett
who through introducing the
First Artist of the Screen to
his precocious, emotional,
and affectionate grand-child, was
directly responsible for what follows

🖎 Acknowledgements

We are greatly indebted to W. Somerset Maugham, who has kindly allowed a passage from A Writer's Notebook, *published by Willliam Heinemann Ltd., to stand as Foreword to this book.*

We desire to express our grateful thanks to Arthur Boulting; Adrian and Christopher Brunel; the Very Reverend the Dean of Canterbury; Robert Florey; Lawrence Gilliam; Raymond Mander and Joe Mitchison (Theatre Collection); Miss Alicia Markova; Ivor Montagu; Paul Rotha; Dr. Eric Saunders; the late George Bernard Shaw; Donald Ogden Stewart; Miss Molly Stoll and Norman Swallow; to all of whom we are indebted for advice and information.

We should also like to record our appreciation of the courtesy and kindness of Miss Gitta Blumenthal (Assistant Curator of the National Film Library); Miss Norah Traylen (Stills Librarian, B.F.I.); and of Harold Brown (Vault Keeper, B.F.I.).

Our thanks also to John Brophy, Thony Christie, Miss Joan Miller, Dr. Robert Niklaus and Mervyn Reeves, who read the first draft of the manuscript, and whose criticism was invaluable.

Contents

Foreword

CHARLIE CHAPLIN. HE IS OF AN AGREEABLE EXTERIOR. HE HAS A NEAT figure, admirably proportioned; his hands and feet are well-shaped and small. His features are good: the nose rather large, the mouth expressive and the eyes fine. His dark hair, touched with white, is waving and abundant. His movements are singularly graceful. He is shy. His speech has in it still a hint of the Cockney of his early youth. His spirits are ebullient. In a company in which he feels himself at ease he will play the fool with a delightful abandon. His invention is fertile, his vivacity unfailing, and he has a pleasant gift of mimicry: without knowing a word of French or Spanish he will imitate persons speaking in one or the other of those languages with a humorous accuracy which is wildly diverting. He will extemporize dialogues between a couple of women in the Lambeth slums which are at once grotesque and moving. Like all humour they depend on a close observation, and their realism, with all its implications, is tragic; for they suggest too near an acquaintance with poverty and squalor. Then he will imitate the various performers in a music-hall of twenty years ago or the amateurs at a cabmen's benefit in a public house on the Walworth Road. But this is mere enumeration: it omits the unbelievable charm that graces all his actions. Charlie Chaplin will keep you laughing for hours on end without effort; he has a genius for the comic. His fun is simple and sweet and spontaneous. And yet all the time you have a feeling that at the back of all is a profound melancholy. He is a creature of moods and it does not require his facetious assertion: "Gee, I had such a fit of the blues last night I didn't hardly know what to do with myself" to warn you that his humour is lined with sadness. He does not give you the impression of a happy man. I have a notion that he suffers from a nostalgia of the slums. The celebrity he enjoys, his wealth, imprison him in a way of life in which he finds only constraint. I think he looks back to the freedom of his struggling youth, with its poverty and bitter privation, with a longing which knows it can never be satisfied. To him the streets of southern London are the scene of frolic, gaiety and extravagant adventure. They have to him a reality which the well-kept avenues, bordered with trim houses, in which live the rich, can never possess. I can imagine him going into his own house and wondering what on earth he is doing in this strange man's dwelling. I suspect that the only home he can ever look upon as such is a second-floor back in the Kennington Road. One night I walked with him in Los Angeles and presently our steps took us into the poorest quarter of the city. There were sordid tenement houses and the shabby, gaudy shops in which are sold the various goods that the poor buy from day to day. His face lit up and a buoyant tone came into his voice as he exclaimed: "Say, this is the real life, isn't it? All the rest is just sham."

W. Somerset Maugham.

✒ Preface

"ONE EVENING IN DECEMBER, I WAS COVERING THE SHORT DISTANCE between the theatre and my favourite café, as quickly as I could when, a few yards ahead, I recognized Charlie's familiar back. Instinctively, I slowed down, for I was suddenly filled with an inexpressible melancholy as I became aware of the utter isolation of the most popular man in the world. He was walking slowly along, close to the unlit shop windows; there was a heavy mist, and Charlie, his hands in his pockets, kept up a little rhythmic movement of the elbows as he went along. His footsteps made no sound, his coat collar was turned up, and he was so very small in his big coat that he looked like a child dressed in his father's clothes."

Robert Florey, one of Chaplin's few intimate friends, and an associate director of *Monsieur Verdoux*, wrote the above passage. It is a vivid impression of the lonely little tramp Charlie, who was Chaplin's other self and expressed his terrible solitude. Chaplin's solitude, and his sadness, are undeniable, and though his tempestuous and most troubled years are now behind him, those two factors must go with him to the end, because they are at the core of his personality.

Chaplin is one of Bernard Shaw's "vital geniuses". There was in him from the beginning a passionate enjoyment of being alive, an upsurging stream of inexpressible and inexhaustible vitality and zest that puts him among those creative artists who are exceptionally lyrical, romantic and subjective. He stands with Shakespeare and with Dickens; his genius is of their kind, his expression of it as English as theirs, even though he used a different medium: and his melancholy is theirs.

He and Dickens particularly are of the same stock, filled with the same humanism, the same passionate pity for the underdog, the same blaze of anger against persecution, exploitation and injustice. They share too the same ingenuous sentimentality, the gift of pathos exploited until it trembles on the edge of anti-climax, without ever quite falling over; the same keen eye for grotesque or endearing characteristics, the same tremendous feeling for outcast children. Jo the crossing sweeper, Oliver Twist and Smike are blood brothers of the Kid, indeed of Charlie himself. Dora and little Nell, Florence Dombey, Em'ly and their many prototypes walk through Chaplin's films and their simulacra through his life. Both Charles Dickens and Charles Chaplin express the same spontaneous, turbulent genius that is vulgar in the true and best sense of the word. It is their natural outpouring, unchecked, full of gusto and savour, streaked with great faults, accessible to all mankind, life blood transmuted into art.

Chaplin is the Dickens of the film world, with a dash of Shakespeare's ardour, poetry, and universal significance.

Very little is lacking in that film world, except genius. Chaplin, in his own person, supplied that lack in several capacities. Actor, comedian, mime, dancer, producer, director, script-writer, musician, composer, conductor and business man, his total control of his work brought about a unique achievement.

In his films, from the Keystone Comedies of 1914 to *Monsieur Verdoux* in 1947, Chaplin has presented in its nakedness his own personality and the core of his artistry. Chaplin and Charlie grew up together. There has been throughout an intimate relation between the man and his work, the creator and the created. And Charlie, so much a projection of his creator, became a universal figure, recognized by all nations and races, accepted and understood by every heart.

Chaplin, in common with all who cannot be brought into the herd, is much loved and much hated, and the clue to it all is in his work. We, who are among those who love Charlie and admire Chaplin, undertook this book in the hope of reviving old memories, and helping to bring about a greater understanding of a very great man.

PART ONE CHAPLIN'S LIFE

✍ Background to Genius

IN THE YEAR 1889, TWO EVENTS TOOK PLACE, ONE OF WORLD WIDE interest, the other of interest to very few people indeed. In America, Thomas Alva Edison invented the Kinetoscope, ancestor of the motion-picture camera; and in England an obscure music-hall artist, Hannah Chaplin, gave birth to a son, Charles, destined to become the greatest exponent of the art of film.

If, as Hamlet insisted, "there is a destiny that shapes our ends, rough hew them how we will", this coincidence is extremely interesting. In the years following Edison's invention, a great film industry was established and organized in America, while the young Chaplin struggled for survival against all the vicissitudes of poverty. It was not until 1913 that the young Cockney lad entered the world of film and, in a remarkably short space of time, made it his own.

Charlie Chaplin was born into a theatrical background. His father, Charles Chaplin senior, was a singer well known to the music hall public of the eighties. He was an amiable person, with a considerable knowledge of music, and a versatility that allowed him to take part in straight plays whenever opportunity offered. He used to boast that in his time he had played every character known to the English stage. Certainly he did not reach the greatest heights, either in the theatre or on the halls; and all that remains of his temporary popularity is his likeness, in topper and dress coat, on the cover of a nineteenth century music sheet—*Pals that time cannot alter.*

His wife, Hannah, was also a small time artist and a singer, appearing under the name Lily Harley. She had taken leading rôles in stock companies performing Gilbert and Sullivan operas, and had also toured the halls as a singer and dancer in vaudeville. At the time of Chaplin's birth, his parents were touring their own act, and as soon as it was humanly possible, they set off again, taking with them the new baby and his two-year-old half-brother Sydney.

It was not an easy life for those young parents. There was always anxiety about future bookings, the wear and tear of continually moving from one place to another, the dreariness of indifferent lodgings, the discomfort and difficulty of life on tour with very young children. Hannah, taking a hurried last look at the sleeping baby dumped in a corner of the crowded dressing room before she went on, must often have longed for a more stable existence.

The earliest tragedy to touch Chaplin was his father's death. He has told how he stood all night long outside St. Thomas' Hospital, watching the light that shone from the unshuttered window of the ward where he knew his father to be, locked in the desolation and terror of the very small child who is aware of catastrophe impending without knowing its nature or cause.

With the death of his father came absolute penury. Hannah, until now the driving force of the little family, stronger than her gentle, ineffectual husband to carry the burdens of existence, lost heart with his going. She could not accept many professional engagements, because of the children. She had no income, and the problem of maintaining even a moderate standard of living was insoluble.

Chaplin by this time resembled any urchin running wild in Chester Street or Kennington Park or Lambeth Walk. Among the noisy crowd of quarrelling guttersnipes, Charlie held his own—an undersized child covered with the grime and filth of the streets and gutters of Lambeth, possessor of a raucous Cockney voice that could shout all others down.

Like most youngsters, he led a dual existence. Outside, there was all the excitement of gang warfare, of inciting his playmates like a young Napoleon against the enemy that lurked in the next backyard. There was the glory of playing hookey from the school he hated, of swimming in the Kennington baths whenever he could afford the entrance-money, of attending the magic lantern shows at the Baxter Hall, where a penny would entitle him to coffee and cake as well as a fascinating exposition of the Crucifixion or the Flight into Egypt. There was the illicit fun of pilfering from street stalls; and there was the stimulus of escaping from the heavy-footed policeman on the beat whenever two of the local toughs started fighting in the middle of the streets, or a stray ball broke a window.

Then there was the endless fascination of the streets and the shops, like bright caverns filled with unimaginable treasure. The hungry little boy pressed his nose against the pastrycook's window, feeding his empty stomach with the warm smell of bread and the sight of succulent cakes and pastries covered with icing and stuffed with fruit and cream. Old bookshops fascinated him even though he could not read. It was enough for him to look at prints and engravings and illustrations for his active imagination to be led into other worlds.

He became a social success among his peers and among his neighbours when it was discovered that he could imitate everyone and everything, from the poor old cabby with the bad feet and boots that were too big for him to the local rent collector who was always swiping ineffectually at the drops hanging perpetually from the end of his nose.

His home life was soberer altogether. Hannah, in her anxiety and growing ill health, treated him as a contemporary. He shared her worries, and her perpetual struggle to make ends meet. There was the closest bond between them, and Charlie suffered with her and for her.

He and Sydney, before childhood was left behind, had earned their living in a multitude of ways. They had both helped their mother with the sewing which brought in a small income. Charlie for a time sold newspapers at Ludgate Circus, running barefoot after customers, trying to increase the number of copies sold. They made toys out of cardboard, wastepaper and matchsticks and sold them to their wealthier friends or to passers by. Charlie was already showing an unusual gift for dancing, and one of their favourite ways of earning money was to follow a barrel-organ man until he reached a pitch. Then Charlie would dance and attract an amused crowd, while Sydney took round the hat. Quick as lightning the children would run off with the money taken, pursued by the cries of the organgrinder who suddenly realized he was to have no share in the profits.

Occasionally some member or another of the little family would get a minor engagement on the halls, and for a few days the spectre of destitution would be put to flight.

In spite of all these efforts, the two boys were nearly always hungry, their lusty appetites cheated with soup from the free soup kitchen, rotten fruit gathered from the gutters into which it was thrown by the stall holders, and odd pennyworths of stale cake. Clothing was sketchy and insufficient, bedding likewise, and sometimes, when all their meagre resources had failed them, they were forced into a midnight flit, taking their few belongings surreptitiously from one shabby room to another even shabbier. If the landlady were shrewd enough to suspect what they were planning, she would put a distraint upon their goods; and then the new life would begin with only mattresses, to which they were entitled by law, to furnish the new lodging.

The hopelessness of their existence, the relentless anxieties that beset her caused Hannah to have a complete breakdown. Charlie never forgot the horrifying moment when he returned home to find several neighbouring children standing by the house eying him curiously. They told him that his mother had been taken away in an ambulance, and when he rushed up to their room he found it empty.

For a time, Syd and he led the lives of little vagabonds, sleeping in parks, feeding on street refuse, with no one responsible for them, and they responsible to no one. When, however, this state of affairs was discovered by those in authority, the two boys were sent to the Hanwell Institution, a workhouse orphanage for destitute children, where Charlie, who until then had enjoyed the fullest freedom of the streets, found himself behind doors that were barred and bolted against him. That was perhaps the unhappiest period of his early years. Living apart from the mother to whom he was utterly devoted, in conditions different from any he had known before, he pined for his release. And it was a happy day for him when his mother was able to make a home for him again.

Charlie survived his childhood; but the mark of it never left him. He drew upon the experiences and background of those early years to furnish the most poignant episodes of his films—*The Kid* is very largely autobiographical. And Charlie, the little tramp, that comic endearing figure who captured the hearts of three hundred million people, is none other than the boy Charlie, the little hungry gutter urchin, denied everything, who yet had the spirit to conquer adverse circumstances.

In a Transatlantic call to Lambeth which was broadcast on March 5th, 1943, Chaplin gives a vivid picture of the memory left with him of his early days: —

"Although I left Lambeth thirty-five years ago, I shall always remember the top room at 3, Pownall Terrace, where I lived as a boy; I shall always remember climbing up and down those three flights of narrow stairs to empty those troublesome slops. Yes, and Heeley's, the greengrocer's in Chester Street, where one could purchase fourteen pounds of coal and a pennorth of pot herbs and a pound of tuppenny pieces at Waghorn's the butchers; and Ash's the grocer's where one bought a pennyworth of mixed stale cake, with all its pleasant and dubious surprises.

"Yes, I went back and visited that little top room in Pownall Terrace, where I had to lug the slops and fourteen pounds of coal. It was all there, the same Lambeth I left, the same squalor and poverty. Now they tell me that Pownall Terrace is ruined, is in ruins, blasted out of existence by the German blitz.

"I remember the Lambeth streets, the New Cut and the Lambeth Walk, Vauxhall Road. They were hard streets, and one couldn't say they were paved with gold, nevertheless the people who lived there are made of pretty good metal."

That was his background as a child, calculated to reduce anyone enduring it to the condition of "inertia that comes of lost hope", a phrase Chaplin uses in describing an old blind man known to him in those days. But Charlie was no ordinary urchin, and the basis of his future work arose from the unpromising elements surrounding his early days.

The Artist Emerging

IT WAS INEVITABLE THAT SOONER OR LATER CHAPLIN SHOULD ENTER the world of entertainment in search of a living; and, given the destitution of his family, that his entry should be an early one.

His short spells as newsboy, toymaker and lather boy in a barber's shop brought little profit; while it was clear almost from babyhood that he had unusual gifts.

The hours he spent in closest companionship with his mother fostered and developed his native gift for mimicry and dancing. To entertain her when she was depressed, he would clown and play the fool, growing beside himself with delight as he saw her sadness disappearing before his buffoonery. At that time, it was something urgent and spontaneous, the same impulse which made him mimic various neighbours, or dance fantastic measures with a sober face until his playmates laughed themselves silly and urged him on to wilder mockery. In the opinion of the neighbourhood "that kid Charlie was a reg'lar caution". And never more so than when he was trying to coax his mother out of the blackness of despair.

She, the professional, recognized a real talent, seized upon it and trained it, giving him a basis of technique while he was still almost a baby. She was herself a skilled mimic, and the child spent happy hours with her, as she looked out of their small window, commenting on the passers by, aping their idiosyncrasies and unconsciously opening her son's eyes to the amazing variety of humankind, and its basic sameness.

She still had her professional contacts. The older brother, Sydney, had already had one or two engagements, through her agents. As soon therefore as she felt Charlie was ready for a professional appearance, she secured for him a place among the Eight Lancashire Lads, a troupe of child clog dancers. By the time he was eight years old, he was already a veteran of the troupe, and had appeared in most music-halls in the north of England.

No laws then protected the child performer; and when we bear in mind the fact that as recently as 1948, British Equity, the actors' Trade Union, disclosed the iniquitous underpayment and treatment of child performers in many entertainment centres, it will take little imagination to envisage the conditions governing the life and work of this eight-year-old at the end of the last century—the fifth or sixth share of a bed with dingy, often verminous sheets; the poor food; the long hours of work—travelling, rehearsing, the two or three shows daily. It was a gruelling apprenticeship and serves to show that Chaplin achieved his earliest theatrical experience the hardest way possible.

He was still a member of the troupe in 1899, when he was ten years old, and a seasoned trouper.

In the theatre records of the period, the name Charles Chaplin crops up here and there, at the foot of a variety bill, or against a very minor juvenile rôle.

He was present on two historic occasions. On January 15th, 1900, the London Hippodrome, which had previously been a circus, was opened as a theatre, and the eleven year old Chaplin took a small part in a sketch called *Giddy Ostend*. Four years later he was one of the wolves in the first performance of *Peter Pan* at the Duke of York's on December 27th, 1904.

Between these events, he had played the boy Billy in *Sherlock Holmes*, had toured the provinces with *A Romance of Cockayne* and then returned to London to resume the part of Billy in a revival of *Sherlock Holmes*. There is a revealing anecdote in connection with the last-named play. Chaplin was eleven when he first played Billy. When Gillette handed him the script of his part, he dared not confess to the management that he could neither read nor write, for fear of losing his chance. He took the part home with him, and sat up all night with his mother, who taught it to him word by word.

At fifteen, Chaplin was an experienced professional, accustomed to all the rigours of life on tour, familiar with most of the second-rate provincial houses, and some of the leading London theatres. Before he had reached adolescence, seven gruelling years of hard work and harsh experience were behind him.

By 1906, when he was seventeen, he was appearing fairly regularly in music-hall, first as a solo turn with a repertoire of songs that was, to suit the tastes of the time, both tragic and comic; and later as one of a team of slapstick comedians in *Casey's Court*, where he was given opportunities for clowning that he seized upon with both hands.

From his position at the foot of the bill, the young professional absorbed all that music hall could offer, watched other turns, comedians, singers, dancers—stored up impressions, turned his intuitive and untrained mind upon the material to hand, much as the little vagabond, his earlier self, had wandered through the streets of London, alert and open-eyed.

As Chaplin's professional life developed, so did his desire to acquire the graces that so far had been lacking. He was still poor, but not destitute, so that he could begin to affect a shabby elegance. Over the years, he had conquered his illiteracy, which had been due more to schooldays broken into by early theatrical engagements, domestic disaster, and his own reluctance to attend school regularly, than to any lack of intelligence on his part. He spent happy hours browsing

Duke of York's Theatre

ST MARTIN'S LANE WC

Proprietors ... ... Mr & Mrs FRANK WYATT

Sole Lessee and Manager ... ... CHARLES FROHMAN

CHARLES FROHMAN PRESENTS
A DRAMA IN FOUR ACTS
BY A. CONAN DOYLE
AND WILLIAM GILLETTE
ENTITLED

SHERLOCK HOLMES

BEING A HITHERTO UNPUBLISHED EPISODE
IN THE CAREER OF THE GREAT DETECTIVE
AND SHOWING HIS CONNECTION WITH THE

STRANGE CASE OF MISS FAULKNER

CHARACTERS IN THE PLAY	COMPANY APPEARING IN THE CAST
SHERLOCK HOLMES ...	WILLIAM GILLETTE
DOCTOR WATSON	KENNETH RIVINGTON
JOHN FORMAN	EUGENE MAYEUR
SIR EDWARD LEIGHTON ...	REGINALD DANCE
COUNT VON STAHLBURG	FREDERICK MORRIS
PROFESSOR MORIARTY	GEORGE SUMNER
JAMES LARRABEE ...	FRANCIS CARLYLE
SIDNEY PRINCE ...	QUINTON McPHERSON
ALFRED BASSICK ...	WILLIAM H. DAY
JIM CRAIGIN ...	CHRIS WALKER
THOMAS LEARY ...	HENRY WALTERS
"LIGHTFOOT" McTAGUE ...	WALTER DISON
JOHN ...	THOMAS QUINTON
PARSONS ...	G. MERTON
BILLY	CHARLES CHAPLIN
ALICE FAULKNER ...	MARIE DORO
MRS. FAULKNER	DE OLIA WEBSTER
MADGE LARRABEE ...	ADELAIDE PRINCE
THERESE ...	SYBIL CAMPBELL
MRS. SMEEDLEY ...	ETHEL LORRIMORE

THE PLACE IS LONDON
THE TIME TEN YEARS AGO

FIRST ACT—DRAWING ROOM AT THE LARRABEES'—EVENING

SECOND ACT—SCENE I—PROFESSOR MORIARTY'S
UNDERGROUND OFFICE—MORNING

SCENE II—SHERLOCK HOLMES' APARTMENTS
IN BAKER STREET—EVENING

THIRD ACT—THE STEPNEY GAS CHAMBER—MIDNIGHT

FOURTH ACT—DOCTOR WATSON'S CONSULTING ROOM KENSINGTON—THE
FOLLOWING EVENING

SCENERY BY ERNEST GROS   INCIDENTAL MUSIC BY WILLIAM FURST

INTERMISSIONS

Between the 1st and 2nd Acts, 9 minutes
Between the 2nd and 3rd Acts, 7 minutes
Between the 3rd and 4th Acts, 8 minutes

MATINEE every Saturday at 2.15 o'clock

BUSINESS MANAGER—JAMES W MATHEWS   ACTING MANAGER—ROBERT M EBERLE
STAGE MANAGER—WILLIAM POSTANCE   MUSICAL DIRECTOR—JOHN CROOK

ICES TEA AND COFFEE can be had of the Attendants

*The programme of the revival of Sherlock Holmes, in
which Chaplin played the part of Billy*

over the shabby volumes in second-hand booksellers, in trying to fill the vast gaps in his mind, to understand, immediately and finally, the riddle of the universe.

Every penny he could spare went on gallery seats—at Daly's where he was enchanted with the young Marie Tempest; in the local music-halls, where he studied the turns of the comedians, quickly learning their patter and their songs, mastering any new dance steps that came along with unusual ease. He climbed the gallery to hang upon Beerbohm Tree's performance in Shakespeare's plays; only to imitate him afterwards, to the huge delight of the players and music-hall artists who visited Kennington, among whom he now mixed as an old hand.

About this time, two major experiences came to him—his first love affair, and his discovery of music.

He fell in love with Hetty Kelly, the sister of an old friend. It was a charming boy and girl affair, that came to nothing. They walked together in Kennington Park, sat and talked together of all they would do in the future stretching its shining years ahead, and behaved generally as all young creatures do when first love opens magic casements for them. Perhaps it was nostalgia for the elusive Hetty that later sent Charlie the little tramp in eternal and unavailing pursuit of his lovely blonde, always played in Chaplin's early films by Edna Purviance.

Certainly her memory stayed with him, when the memory of countless others had faded and gone. On his return to London, at the height of his universal fame, he enquired after Hetty, only to learn that she had died two years before. When he took his solitary pilgrimage to the haunts of his childhood, he came to Kennington Park and found there the ghost of the nineteen-year-old boy, dressed to kill, waiting eagerly for the first glimpse of Hetty. The trams still clanged by; but no Hetty in her fresh print dress and her new hat descended from them. She was gone, as the boy was gone, and there was left an aching nostalgia that made Chaplin, writing of the incident later, cry out "Kennington Park! How depressing Kennington Park is! How depressing to me are all parks! The loneliness of them. One never goes to a park unless one is lonesome. And lonesomeness is sad. The symbol of sadness, that's a park".

Chaplin the artist was emerging all the time, in his work, in his thirst for knowledge, and in his reaction to the experiences that came to him. His discovery of music is a case in point. For he made it through hearing, at Kennington Cross, the distant playing of a harmonica and clarinet. The melody was a popular one of the day:

"You are the honey, honeysuckle, I am the bee,

I'd like to sip the honey, dear, from those red lips. You see
I love you dearly, dearly, and I want you to love me.
You are my honey, honeysuckle, I am your bee,—"

as hackneyed then as any that is now daily plugged upon the radio.
But that does not alter the validity of the experience. To the boy
Chaplin it was a haunting message of transcendent beauty, a revelation of a whole mode of expression he had never dreamed existed,
which gave him an instinctive understanding of music. From that
moment of impact, music became one of the important influences in
his life, a solace, a relaxation, as well as an added factor in his
career. It is curious that the distant echoes of two street performers
should set so much in train.

While Charlie was entirely taken up with all the ramifications of
his profession and his private life, Syd unconsciously added a new
and glittering thread to his younger brother's web of destiny. Syd,
after earlier abortive attempts to make his own and the family's
fortune, had been engaged by one Fred Karno, at the princely starting
salary of £3 per week. Syd was by now a clever comedian, and
Karno was abundantly satisfied with his work. It was this fact that
gave Syd enough courage to beg an audition for his kid brother.
It is clear that at this period of their lives, Syd still felt some responsibility for his brother, and was therefore eager to secure an
engagement for him in a company where working conditions were
good, under a management that was extremely well known and very
highly respected.

Up to this moment, Charlie's career had been a matter of chance.
Now Fate, in the guise first of Syd, then of Fred Karno, stepped in;
and from that moment, Charlie's future was inevitable.

✎ The Influence of Fred Karno

FRED KARNO WAS ONE OF THE OUTSTANDING THEATRICAL FIGURES
of the early part of this century. Through winning an amateur contest,
he began his career as an acrobat; then later became one of the most
famous impresarios of his time. He was a born man of the theatre,
with a natural flair for publicity, an ability to give the public what
it wants when it wants it, and an immediate perception of potential
talent. Among those who owe their discovery to him, and indeed
the basis of their art, were Billy Bennett, Sydney and Charles
Chaplin, George Carney, Billy Danvers, Mark Daly, Flanagan and
Allen, Gene Gerrard, Will Hay, Sydney Howard, Bobby Howes, Fred
Kitchen, Max Miller and Naughton and Gold.

In his Fun Factory in Camberwell—"three tall, gaunt, converted houses near Loughborough Junction"—sets, costumes, and props were made for the companies of acrobats, mimes, comedians and singers who went forth every night in Karno's special buses to do the rounds of the music-halls. His shows became the fashion, his name was on everyone's lips, and music-hall artists reached the summit of their dreams when they were engaged by Karno.

His early work as impresario—the famous sketches *Hilarity, Jail Birds, Early Birds, The New Woman's Club,* and those he directed subsequently—derived from the Italian mime that reached its zenith with the Comédie Italienne in France in the seventeenth and eighteenth centuries, and that gave rise to the figures of Harlequin, Columbine, Pantaloon, and Clown in the English pantomime of the nineteenth century. The sketches were improvised, mimed, and filled with knockabout farce—drunks, clowns, custard pies, whitewash and stepladders. A considerable part of the special humour of Karno's sketches lay in the absurdity of the trick that doesn't quite come off—the conjuror who never makes it, the singer who prepares ostentatiously to sing, and then cannot utter a note, the billiards player whose cue never comes into contact with the ball, the drunk who never quite manages to climb down on to the stage from his box. For the rest, Karno's companies were famous for their skill and precision in pace, timing and team work, and for the excellence of their production.

By 1907, when Chaplin's path crossed that of Karno, the Fun Factory at Camberwell was churning out unlimited sketches from mimed slapstick through burlesques with song and dance like *Saturday to Monday* or *Wakes Week,* to musical farces like *Cherry Blossom* or *A Tragedy of Eros,* together with short plays and full length pantomimes. The world-famous sketch *Mumming Birds* had been launched on its colossal run, that was to remain unequalled in the history of music-hall; and in Hollywood, a certain Mack Sennett, engaged in making comedy films, was offering handsome contracts to any of Karno's comedians who entered America as members of Karno's troupes touring abroad.

Karno consented to see Chaplin because of Syd's urgency, and found him at first sight disappointing, as he reported afterwards: "Syd brought his kid brother along—a pale, puny, sullen-looking youngster. I must say that when I first saw him, I thought he looked much too shy to do any good in the theatre, particularly in the knockabout comedies that were my speciality."

Karno watched his new recruit closely, but soon discovered that professionally he was an asset. Chaplin's gift for clowning and mime, his dramatic facility, and the muscular dexterity he had acquired through his prentice years, were all factors contributing to his immediate success in Karno's troupe of comedians. But socially it was another picture. "He wasn't very likeable". Karno admitted ruefully, "I've known him go whole weeks without saying a word to anyone in the company. Occasionally he would be quite chatty, but on the whole he was dour and unsociable. He lived like a monk, had a horror of drink, and put most of his salary away in the bank as soon as he got it."

This weedy, silent seventeen-year-old, is exactly what we should expect at this stage. Charlie was still suffering from the physical strain of his burdened childhood and poverty-stricken adolescence. So far, no real release had been found for his unusual talents; and his catholic reading at this time—politics, economics, philosophy, Schopenhauer and Shakespeare, a little medical science and some history—was an absorbing and indigestible medley for his vividly intelligent mind.

The first sketch of Fred Karno's in which the boy Chaplin was given a part specially made for him was called *The Football Match*. He played a melodramatic villain whose fell purpose it was to bribe the goalkeeper, Harry Weldon, with untold wealth and unlimited drink, to sell the match. He wore a slouch hat and a vast cloak à la Guy Fawkes and—historical moment!—a little black moustache.

His work in this sketch made Karno offer him the principal part in a new show, *Jimmy the Fearless*: and no one was more astonished than Karno when this unfledged member of his company showed no eagerness to seize a chance that any other promising young comedian would have jumped at. Whether through nervousness or through a genuine lack of interest in that particular part, Chaplin hedged to such a degree that Karno, a little piqued, offered it to another boy in the company, Stanley Jefferson, who subsequently became Stan Laurel, of Laurel and Hardy fame.

The young Jefferson made a great success of the part, and later, when he was transferred to another of Karno's companies, Chaplin gladly accepted the role Karno had originally intended for him, and gave it for the first time at the Alhambra, Bradford.

The sketch was concerned with the heroic dream exploits of a working-class lad, and Chaplin, by now finding his artistic feet, was able to add to its presentation comedy business of a kind recognized later in his earliest films.

It is impossible to over-estimate the importance of the years Chaplin was with Karno; and the influence of those years made its mark upon the whole of his subsequent film work, to such a degree that in his latest film to date, *Monsieur Verdoux* (1947), there are moments that derive from the Karno background—Verdoux's unexpected disappearance through a window, his brilliant juggling with cup and saucer while he flings himself quite literally at the feet of his next victim, his abortive attempts in a boat to strangle Martha Raye.

Karno's was a school entirely suited to Chaplin's gifts. Farce is one of the most fertile sources of comedy and in Karno's shows it reached its zenith of inventiveness. Every potentiality of Chaplin was exercised during those enriching years, so that later, part of his great originality was due to the use he made of the situations devised by Karno in his music-hall sketches. He was able, through his genius, to lift that humour to another plane, change the quality of the laughter that was evoked by it. His apprenticeship with Karno gave him the germ of many of his early films; his genius caused that germ to develop along lines that are best shown in the difference between the entertaining but stock figure of Jimmy the Fearless, and Charlie the little tramp, who embodied all mankind.

Moreover, the wide scope of Karno's repertoire—which resembled more than anything else the vaudeville shows given in the little boîtes dotted here and there along the boulevards of Paris, where pathos and satire, drama and idyll, melancholy and gaiety go hand-in-hand—added to Chaplin's versatility, while the high standards Karno demanded of his companies gave him polish and finesse as well as adding to his considerable technique.

Chaplin's career was, in this sense, launched by Fred Karno, who had launched so many celebrities, but none greater than the "sullen-looking youngster" Syd Chaplin brought along. There is no doubt that his early years in films achieved their incredible momentum because of the years with Karno that had preceded them.

There was another factor of importance. While the young Chaplin was developing his unusual talent under the ægis of Karno, Mack Sennett in Hollywood was still signing up as many Karno-trained comedians as would come, absorbing them into the similar ritual of his *Keystone Coppers* series with Ford Sterling. To have been with Karno was a passport to the magical and dollar-laden world of film; and Chaplin had his passport before ever he set foot in America!

✍ Pioneer Days in Film

BY THE TIME CHAPLIN WAS EXPERIENCED ENOUGH TO TAKE OVER major rôles in Karno's sketches, a difficult position had arisen concerning Karno's American companies, which toured similar programmes all over the United States and Canada under the management of Alfred Reeves.

In 1910, Hollywood was stretching out rapacious arms to clutch at any actor or actress on the legitimate stage who might prove to be the stuff from which film stars are made overnight. In particular, there was a dearth of comedians.

At this very early stage in film making there was no attempt to do more than turn the camera on a group of players using their normal stage technique. Film comedians were required to indulge in knockabout farce, as they would do in vaudeville or on the halls.

Fred Karno's artistes, superbly trained, exactly filled Hollywood's bill, with the result that every few weeks, Karno lost another of his American company. Film contracts at undreamed of salaries dazzled them and swept them away, and members of the companies in England were sent out to replace those who entered films. Hollywood's maw was so insatiable that very soon Karno had to decide which of the Chaplin brothers he would send out on an American tour.

The choice fell upon Charlie, for Karno found Syd invaluable, and wanted to keep him in England. He called the boy into his office to tell him of his new position, at a salary of £15 per week, a salary so princely that Charlie, just twenty-one, stared at him open-mouthed, and listened in stupefied silence while Karno reminded him of the fair conditions of work he always offered, of the way in which Charlie himself had been given every chance to develop his talent and reach the highest rungs of his profession. Karno then outlined the situation that had arisen in the United States, and urged Charlie to remember that he owed a certain loyalty to his employer: "Now look here, Charlie—see you don't go and do the same as the others. A fat contract can be tempting, but I've always been fair to you, now see you're fair to me."

Charlie came out of his stupor to say very earnestly, and with absolute sincerity: "Don't worry, Guv'nor! I can't see myself trying to be funny in front of a camera. Not up my street at all!"

This certainty on his part helped him to resist the blandishments of the Hollywood scouts on the occasion of his first American tour. But it was also true that three years before, when he had been sent with one of Karno's companies to Paris, where he appeared at the

Cigale, and the Folies Bergères, he had seen some of Max Linder's films and had been enormously impressed by Linder's use of comedy technique. Now, on this first American tour, though he had not felt any desire to enter films himself, he was fascinated by the making of films when he came into contact with some of the pioneers who were groping their way towards a fuller realization of the new form of entertainment.

Curiously enough, his own first film appearance was made just before he set out on his second, and fateful, tour of the States and Canada. He was at the time touring the Channel Islands, in August, 1912; and it was in Jersey that a news cameraman, filming a carnival procession, included Chaplin in his shot of the crowd looking on.

Two months later, he was on his way to America. While others of the company gossiped and gambled, flirted and played other deck games, Charlie mooched around by himself, leaning over the rails and staring into space or wrapping himself up in a remote corner to read or dream. The other members of the company were used to it, as they were used to his occasional wild bursts of noisy gaiety. He was a trouper, and he had his points even if he was inclined to go off by himself too much.

Perhaps this time his desire for solitude came from a realization of changes pending, for later he described how he felt when the boat docked. "I shall never forget the extraordinary emotion I felt when the boat drew alongside the docks of New York. There we stood, fourteen young Englishmen. And I'm sure I was moved more than any of the others. I realized intuitively that I was going to achieve my destiny in America. I had so profound an inward assurance of this that I had to tell the others, with all the over-emphasis and conceit of callow youth. Raising my arm in salute to New York, I yelled "I give you fair warning, America! I'm coming to conquer you!"

Charlie was always good at histrionics, and this gesture must have amused his companions, and satisfied Charlie's sense of drama, though even he was not aware that his utterance was prophetic.

The story of Chaplin's discovery by Mack Sennett—if indeed it was Mack Sennett and not his director, Adam Kessel—has achieved its legendary trimmings. There is however a persistent thread linking the several versions and it does seem more than probable that Chaplin owed his entry into films to the intransigeance of Ford Sterling, at that time Sennett's leading man. Sterling, aware of the shortage of film comedians and the increasing popularity of comic films, made frequent demands for bigger and better contracts with fabulous salaries attached to them. Sennett, growing progressively more tired of these excessive and persistent demands, looked about him for someone to replace Sterling.

It was with all this in mind that he one day entered Pantage's Theater in Los Angeles, at a time when the management had booked one of Karno's companies. It so happened that the world-famous *Mumming Birds* was being shown. None of the characters in this sketch, which was given in America under the title of *A Night in a London Music-Hall*, had any names. Some were performers—a conjuror, a singer, a soubrette, a dramatic actor, and so forth—while others—the drunken dude, the dear old Uncle, the mischievous lad in the box—pretended to be members of the audience interfering with the performance, or manifesting their disapproval of it in various ways. When Sennett saw the sketch the young Chaplin, following in the footsteps of a long line of distinguished comedians, was playing the drunken reveller who hurled abuse and vegetables upon the performers, and who was always on the point of falling out of the box, from which vantage point he was supposed to be watching the show.

Chaplin made such an impression on Mack Sennett that when increasing dissatisfaction with Ford Sterling compelled him to think seriously of doing without him, he sent the now famous wire to Adam Kessel, his director in New York: "Try to get hold of a bloke called Chapman, Caplin, or something, playing second circuit."

Mack Sennett was at that time the director of Keystone Productions in Los Angeles, a branch of the New York Motion Picture Company. Bert Ennis was the manager of the company, and to him therefore fell the duty of raking America for the bloke called Chapman or Caplin. After several days spent going through recent numbers of theatre magazines—the *Clipper*, the *Billboard* and *Variety*, where he drew a blank, Ennis received news from his brother on the *Billboard* staff, that the comedian he was seeking was a leading man in one of Karno's companies, and playing Philadelphia. Ennis therefore cabled Alfred Reeves, who was able to give him all the details concerning the elusive "Caplin".

Even then, Chaplin's entry into the film world was delayed while he hesitated to exchange the security of his work with Karno for an uncertain future in an unknown medium. The first offer made him was seventy-five dollars a week; but though he was tempted —he who had known and feared poverty—he still dared not take so enormous a risk. But the New York Motion Picture Company was determined to get Chaplin, and after considerable delay due to hesitation on both sides, Chaplin finally accepted a year's contract at one hundred and twenty-five dollars a week—nearly three times as much as he was earning with Karno—to make films under the direction of Mack Sennett.

Chaplin arrived in Los Angeles not knowing a soul there, except the door-keeper of a theatre where he had once played with the Karno troupe. It was typical of him to take a cheap room in an hotel just opposite that theatre. He then informed Mack Sennett of his arrival, but could not summon up enough courage to go to the studio and present himself to his new employer. A whole week went by before Chaplin could force himself to enter the studio. When he did, Sennett at once put him at ease, and advised him to wander round for a few days, and get used to the studio and its atmosphere.

It seemed, when Chaplin made his first diffident entry into the alien world of the studio, that his engagement there was a catastrophe. His first few weeks were lonely and unhappy. The atmosphere was hostile to him, the manner of working antipathetic, and the company clearly regarded him as an intruder. Directors found no work for him; his colleagues watched him closely but did not speak to him, so that, plunged in gloom, he presented badly both professionally and socially, just as he had when he first became a member of Karno's company.

Mack Sennett, who had staked everything on finding in Chaplin a worthy successor to Ford Sterling, must have been profoundly worried. "It was weeks", he said later, "before Charlie put over anything real. He tried all sorts of make-ups—one of them I remember was a fat man—and they were all about equally flat. As a matter of fact, for some time I felt more than a little uneasy as to whether my find was a very fortunate one!"

But gradually Chaplin found his feet—not only metaphorically, but actually. For from the moment he put on the costume of the little tramp with the enormous out-turned boots, he began to feel at ease before the camera, and to develop lines of comedy that made his colleagues look at him with respect.

In those early days, the Sennett studio was a small and informal place. Every member of the company shared in all the chores of film making from acting to cutting and washing the film strips. The small and primitive dressing rooms were social clubs, where everything under the sun could be endlessly discussed.

One of the most important factors in Chaplin's new life was Mabel Normand, Sennett's leading lady, and a very fine comedienne. She was the first person to show any friendliness to the lonely young man, and the first to give him confidence in his abilities in film. She was herself a fine enough artist to realize that Chaplin could not at first find his own approach to the new medium, trammelled as it already was by an almost inflexible conception of humour—that of slapstick farce, which Chaplin had already left a long way behind. She was also the first to see that when he did find his own line, he brought with him an entirely new form of imaginative comedy infinitely more subtle than anything yet known in comic films.

Mabel Normand's dressing room was the only one that possessed an oil stove. And there, for hours on end, the twenty-three year old Chaplin in his natty checked suit would discuss with her their work, their future, life and art and books and all those things his mind had been filled with through the years of his adolescence. The others listened and commented, but it was Mabel's mind that matched his own, and to her he was speaking. Those were some of the happiest hours of his life, and though his work with her was tinged with a faint feeling of rivalry—she was more experienced in film work, and had an excellent comedy technique of her own, and was in addition a beautiful and vivacious girl—he enjoyed it, and made an excellent foil for her.

But even Mabel's affection was sorely tried the day Sennett decided they should be filmed riding a motor-cycle, provided Charlie knew how to ride one.

"Of course I do!" Charlie asserted scornfully. "I used to cycle all over London. What are you worrying about?"

He mounted the motor-cycle, Mabel jumped on the pillion; and then the horrified onlookers saw the pair of them whizzing down a steep hill with the speed of an express train. It was perfectly clear that Charlie could not guide nor control nor stop the machine.

No one knows what Charlie thought about as he hurtled down to destruction. Behind him, Mabel clung on grimly, her eyes closed against the terror of whirling trees and hedges and the inevitable doom. It came.

Mabel was thrown headlong into a ditch; Charlie, battered and bruised, was discovered spreadeagled a few yards further along the the road. By a miracle, both escaped serious injury, and only the motor-cycle succumbed. Charlie's excuse, when he could speak, was that he hadn't realized there was any difference between a cycle and a motor-cycle.

Fame and Fortune

MACK SENNETT'S CONTRIBUTION TO THE PIONEERING OF FILM comedy was unique. He, more than any other in America, increasingly moved from the theatrical representation of vaudeville skit and slapstick farce towards the cinematic use of gesture, movement, and shape. After a study of the work of Max Linder and Lucca in France, he had left the Biograph Studio to become director of the Keystone Productions.

Once established, he began to put into practice the theories he had derived from the Continental school of film making, and produced comedies that were original in their blending of charm with burlesque —his Bathing Beauties and his Keystone Cops were symbolic of this blending.

The Keystone Comedians, like those trained by Karno, drew upon the earliest essences of comedy for their effects—misunderstandings, disguises, enormous effort exerted for a result that never came off, violent anger over incidents that had never taken place, imagined slights that led to chaos, incongruity of person or situation. The sources of their comedy went back to the earliest known form of theatre; and that was the secret of their universal popularity, and the reason why Sennett found in Karno's comedians all that he wished for in his own.

If Chaplin's first slice of luck in his career was his engagement by Karno, the second certainly was his work with Sennett. The latter, himself an innovator, allowed Chaplin to evolve his own line to a remarkable degree, always, of course, within the existing framework of the Keystone Comedy.

In the year he spent at the Keystone Studio, Chaplin acquired the rudiments of his own special brand of comedy in terms of film; and, slowly, Charlie the little tramp began to emerge. One by one the endearing mannerisms crept in—the vertical salute of the little bowler hat, the turned-out feet, the trick of throwing a cigarette end over his shoulder and kicking it away. Both these last were taken from Fred Kitchen, a fine music-hall comedian who was also Karno-trained, and whom Chaplin watched with interest in his youth.*

---

* Fred Kitchen died on April 1st, 1951. Footnote quotation from *The Stage* newspaper of April 5th, 1951:

One of the few remaining links with the old-time music-hall has gone with the death, last Sunday, of Fred Kitchen. Mr. Kitchen, who was 77 and died in a Hampton-hill nursing home, was discovered by Fred Karno more than fifty years ago. Large-hearted in his generosity of feeling and big physically, Fred Kitchen was the originator the catch-phrase "Meredith, we're in!"—the last line of his famous music-hall sketch, "Moses and Son", which he toured for many years. He became a leading comedian for Fred Karno. He claimed to be the first comedian to wear outsize boots, and when asked why he never played in America, replied that everyone there would say he was imitating Charlie Chaplin.

It was Mr. Kitchen who helped Chaplin when the Kennington boy was setting out on his professional career. Fred Kitchen, a master of mime himself, taught Chaplin the rudiments of this art. At seven he was earning a few shillings a week. But by 1918 his salary was £450 a week for appearances at the Folies Bergère in Paris. He did not often appear in the

By the time his year at Keystone was ended, Chaplin had made thirty-five comic films, conquered the American screen, found his artistic feet, and was possessed of an urgent desire to direct his own films.

The beginning of 1915 found him with the Essanay Company, who had offered him one thousand dollars a week. The agent offering the contract was astounded to hear him demand a thousand and seventy-five. It was such an odd sum that the agent, case-hardened though he must have been, asked why he wanted just that much.

"I need the extra seventy-five to live on", said Chaplin, as though explaining everything.

"And the thousand?"

"That's to go into safe bonds."

His terror of a sudden return to the poverty he had known and escaped from was so acute that he intended to put away a thousand dollars every week. He did not believe that such good fortune as had already come his way could possibly last, he had no faith in his capacity to go on earning at such a rate; and he had calculated that a year at the salary offered by Essanay would save him from the worst menaces of poverty for the rest of his life if he invested his savings wisely. That was why he demanded the extra seventy-five to live on.

In the fourteen films he made with Essanay, Chaplin developed along the lines he had already laid down. Charlie the little tramp was already established in the affections of the film-going public. Chaplin now for the first time added an undercurrent of pathos to the absurd adventures of his film self; and the public found him still more endearing.

West End, the provinces being his theatre-home, but his gift as a player of sketches, his power to bring tears to the eyes of his audiences, and his robust, clean humour were celebrated throughout the world of music-hall.

After he retired, in 1945, Mr. Kitchen seldom went to the theatre, though he continued to take a lively interest in his fellow-artists. He was one of the oldest members of the Grand Order of Water Rats. Mr. Kitchen expressed a wish that the words, "Meredith, we're in", should be engraved on his tombstone, which, it is understood, is to be done.

Fred Kitchen, one of a family connected with the stage for more than a century, was born in 1873. His first appearance was at the Prince's, Portsmouth, when he was carried on to the stage in his father's arms in "The Dumb Man of Manchester". His first important part was as a pageboy in "His Majesty's Guest", at the Princess's, Glasgow. He had a remarkable gift for touching his audiences with his depth of pathos, and was said to be one of the few actors able to cry real tears on the stage. There was a benefit for him at the Winter Garden, London, in 1945. Mrs. Kitchen died during the last war.

Fred Kitchen, Junr., his son, carries on the family music-hall tradition, being an artist of personality and talent in his own right.

In one of them, *The Bank*, there is an incident that calls to mind the Karno sketch *Jimmy the Fearless*, in which Chaplin had appeared as a boy. There, the boy Jimmy awakes from his dream just as the heroine welcomes him. In *The Bank* the little janitor Charlie awakes from a similar dream of heroic deeds just as he is about to embrace his beloved; and finds himself kissing a mop.

Chaplin by now, at the age of twenty-seven, and after only two years in films, was the most sought-after comedian in Hollywood, and had proved himself the Essanay company's most valuable asset.

At the end of the year, he was offered a new contract at five thousand dollars a week. Chaplin, beside himself with excitement, rushed off to tell the staggering news to his half-brother Sydney, who had followed him to Hollywood.

It was some time before Syd could understand the import of Charlie's incoherent shouting; but when he did, he simply said: "If you take my advice, you'll turn it down."

"Turn it down?"

"You'll be crazy to take it!"

"I'll be crazy if I don't."

"Look—if they offer you five thousand, you can bet your boots you're worth double. Don't be a mug!"

"Are you seriously suggesting I turn down a contract at five times the rate I'm getting already?"

"I'm seriously suggesting you sit down and think it all out, without being had for a sucker! I should have thought you'd learned a bit of business sense by now!"

"So I have! Enough not to turn down a fat contract when I've got my hands on it! Who else is going to offer me terms like this?"

All Charlie's intimates backed Syd's view, but Charlie was terrified of losing such excellent terms when no others might be offered. He was torn between rage at his brother's interference—for Syd forcibly restrained him from getting into contact with the Essanay directors, and set all his friends to watch him, and prevent him signing the contract—and an uneasy fear that Syd was right.

Syd meantime had gone to New York as a self-appointed agent for his brother, to find out which other companies were prepared to make offers. He had the enormous satisfaction of proving himself right, of wiping the rage off his brother's face, and of earning a handsome commission. For Charlie, who never did anything by halves, was now as grateful for the interference as he had previously resented it.

Charlie's new contract, with the Mutual Company, reached the hitherto unknown figure of ten thousand dollars a week, with a bonus

Charles Spencer Chaplin

The unknown music-hall
artiste (*Chaplin on the left*)

Triumphant Return, 1921

Chaplin in Hollywood:
with Douglas Fairbanks, Senior, D. W. Griffiths and Mary Pickford

with Samuel Goldwyn, Mary Pickford and Douglas Fairbanks, Senior

Lita Grey

Paulette Goddard

Oona O'Neill

A Happy Ending?

At a première, with Paulette Goddard and Jackie Cooper

With Orson Welles at a meeting held to support the opening of a Second Front (1942)

"Open a Second Front Now" speech to Europe (1942)

Watching mass picketing by strikers in Hollywood

The Joan Barry Paternity Case (1943). Fingerprints taken

Chaplin *v.* The United States. A word with Counsel

of a hundred and fifty thousand dollars. When he and Syd left the Mutual offices the day the contract was signed, Charlie was so dazed with awe and unbelief that he kept fingering the cheque for a hundred and fifty thousand dollars, as if to make sure that it really existed.

"Let's celebrate! Oh boy! Let's celebrate! There's this, Syd— if they never give me another penny. I'm safe now!"

Then he halted suddenly. "All this money! And I can't think of anything to buy! What a waste!"

The terms of this contract were so unprecedented at that time that Mary Pickford, his friend, and rival for place as first screen favourite, demanded similar terms for reasons of prestige: and film companies generally had no reason to bless the decision of the Mutual Company to offer Chaplin ten times the amount he was previously receiving.

More important still from the point of view of his future, the Mutual contract carried with it artistic freedom. He was to make twelve films yearly, at the rate of one a month; and all the films he made for the company were scripted and directed by himself.

All Charlie's fears and doubts returned in full force the day he first set foot in the Mutual Studio. He had no idea at all for his first film there, no theme, no incident, no inspiration; and the more he sought it, the more it eluded him. Executives, camera staff, actors and actresses were all ready and waiting. He looked at them with sick horror. He had nothing to give them. Nothing at all.

Days passed by. The Mutual director wondered how to face the Board. The company grew bored, then apprehensive. Chaplin, wrapped in impenetrable gloom, paced the studio floor, disappeared into his office; and, when tracked down there by exasperated or desperate executives, was found staring blankly into space, with so unhappy an expression that they withdrew without having said a word.

A whole week had gone by, when Chaplin entered one of the big Los Angeles stores and stood by a counter waiting his turn, watching the customers going up the moving stairway to the next floor. He began to see himself, a floorwalker in the store, trying to run down the stairs that were going up.

Something like a hurricane or a thunderbolt came upon the crowded store. A small dark man bolted through the shoppers, out into the main thoroughfare, jumped into a cab, shouted the address, and talked happily to himself the whole way to the studio.

Before the apathetic company was aware of what had happened, Chaplin was among them. His incredible vitality filled the studio, jerked them all into feverish activity. The lost week behind them for ever, Charlie set them to work upon *The Floorwalker,* one of his funniest Mutual films.

He had brought with him from Essanay Studios the lovely blonde Edna Purviance, whom he had first met early in 1915, when she was secretary to an industrial magnate in San Francisco. Chaplin at length persuaded her to throw in her fortunes with his, and she left the office for the film studio. At first, she was clumsy and self-conscious in her acting, and though in real life she was charming, on the screen she lacked any real personality. But Chaplin, with infinite patience, made an artist of her, and one who responded to his least direction. She played the rôle of the beautiful heroine whom the little tramp Charlie adored from afar, without ever reaching his heart's desire.

Though his reputation was firmly established and he was already known to millions on the screen, Chaplin knew few of the film colony of the time, among whom were numbered Owen Moore, Ruth Roland, D. W. Griffiths, Mabel Normand, Ford Sterling, Ben Turpin, Bessie Barriscale, Dustin Farmer, Charlie Ray, Chester Conklin, Fatty Arbuckle and Mack Swain.

Among his intimates were Mary Pickford and Douglas Fairbanks, Sam Goldwyn and Mack Sennett, whom he saw fairly frequently. For the rest he lived an austere and solitary life in a bare six-roomed house, tended by a Japanese houseboy.

He had not changed much from the morose lad of the Karno days, whose sudden bursts of gaiety, and superlative mimicry had both delighted and astonished his colleagues. Alone in his small house, he plunged into reading, catching up with the lost years. For a time he fell completely under the spell of the free thinkers, and filled his rooms with their pamphlets, booklets, and weightier tomes. He still read politics, economics, and what his friends called "all the gloomier philosophers"—Schopenhauer still keeping his first place. He also developed an inborn gift of being able to speak with authority and distinction on subjects that were not really familiar to him—some years later, on his first visit to Europe, the president of the Bank of England was impressed with his informed views on banking and international finance. None of his intimates knew where such knowledge came from.

Spells of solitude were succeeded by spells of happy sociability, when his vivacity and intelligence always attracted a number of people to him. On those occasions, he was the most excellent companion—witty, ebullient, endearing, and capable of entertaining large gatherings with his spontaneous mimicry—of a classical dancer, a hotel magnate, an old street vendor, a young girl listening to her first proposal. He could keep any group of people enthralled for as long as he chose, his own energy never flagging.

As he reached the peaks, so he touched the depths; and there were days when he neither saw nor spoke to anyone round him, sometimes leaving the studio suddenly and without warning, to spend the day walking all over Hollywood, wrapped in darkness. Sam Goldwyn, famous as much for his astonishingly original use of the English language as for his pioneer work in the cinema, was one of Chaplin's few intimates, and he seems to have understood his complexity with amazing insight. He said of Chaplin: "His reaction to life is, you see, intensely personal, intensely emotional. Chaplin loves to talk about government and economics and religion. When Rupert Hughes came out to Hollywood he and Charlie were much given to what somebody calls 'topics'—just topics. Nothing could have been more illuminating. While Hughes conducted his side of the discussion in a spirit of dispassionate inquiry, the less scientifically trained mind of the comedian struck out with a poet's frenzy at everything which he did not like. One could see it was not really abstract truth which he desired. It was the theory which most successfully represented his own prejudice."

By this time Edna Purviance was so firmly established in Chaplin's life and work that she was accepted without comment or scandal, and soon acquired a number of friends in the film colony, as well as a considerable reputation in films. With the series he made for the Mutual Company, Chaplin not only reached a great peak in his own work and put himself at the head of the film world; but in them he set down some of the fundamental laws of cinema, and comedy in film.

He worked himself to a standstill over every film. When, for example, the shooting of the *Immigrant* was finished, Chaplin spent four days and four nights, without sleep or rest or more than a mouthful of food, cutting and assembling the film, until he was satisfied with it. By which time, more than nine-tenths of the original length had been discarded. When he had finished, he looked like a drunken tramp, dirty, dishevelled, with a four-days' beard, his hair on end, his collar hanging by a thread, his eyes sunken through lack of sleep. He could hardly keep on his feet; but the film was finished.

When his contract with the Mutual company expired, he was inundated with offers from all the major American companies, and Mutual offered him still more favourable terms.

By now, Chaplin was fully aware of his commercial value, and together with his artistry had developed his business acumen. In June, 1917 therefore he accepted the unprecedented conditions offered by the First National Company—the famous million dollar contract for eight films of any length, to be made within eighteen months. So much now was he his own master that early in 1918 he began to build his own studio on La Brea Avenue, where all his subsequent films have been made to date.

At the age of twenty-eight Chaplin was on top of the world, with enough money behind him to scare away the bogey of poverty for ever, with freedom to shape his career according to his own creative impulse, with a loyal and utterly devoted partner in Edna Purviance, and a degree of universal fame and popularity that no one in the history of mankind had ever before achieved.

✑ Marriage and Divorce

CHAPLIN'S POPULARITY WAS DUE IN SOME MEASURE TO THE TIME AT which his first films appeared. The 1914-18 World War was spreading its ugly tentacles over Europe, and reaching out desperately towards America. Soldiers and civilians alike suffered from warfare on a vaster scale than any known before, waged with more lethal weapons, and already engendering far-reaching consequences. Soldiers and civilians alike were enduring the domestic and economic upheaval that comes with war, the personal and social suffering, the monotony and the agony, the frustration and the sorrow.

Charlie was a godsend. His comedy sent a light to pierce the gloom; his absurd and fantastic misfortunes released the mind from greater misfortunes; his pathos was an outlet for grief. He was able to convulse his audiences with healthy, happy laughter. He was a tonic and a katharsis at a time when both were needed.

More than this, the endearing little tramp was Everyman, and when *Shoulder Arms* was released at the end of the war, there was not a soldier who did not recognize the truth of this revelation of the boredom and monotony of war, even while he rocked in his seat with the hilarious comedy it contained; there was not a woman present who did not see, in the lonely little soldier to whom no one wrote nor ever sent a parcel, the heart of the desolation she had endured for so long.

The war itself influenced Chaplin's reputation in another and subtler way. It was impossible for him to have achieved such fame so rapidly without acquiring detractors among his envious competitors; and an insidious campaign began in the press suggesting that Chaplin was skulking in Hollywood, enjoying himself, when he should be at the front. When, in 1917, America entered the war, thousands of angry letters were received, from England and the United States, all indignant because he had not joined up, some even threatening him. And at the same time he was widely denounced in the press. War brings its own hysteria, and people in the public eye always suffer from the malice of their fellow men.

In Chaplin's case, the opprobrium was unmerited. When war was declared, Chaplin and other British members of the studio had immediately volunteered. Nothing happened until Chaplin had pestered the British Ambassador in Washington several times; and then he was not passed by the army doctors.

None of his detractors paid any attention to the facts of the case, and the outcry in the press reached such serious proportions that Chaplin was forced to make a public statement. He did so with a logic and dignity that could not appeal to the prejudices of the war-minded, white-feather patriots, but did reach reasonable and just citizens. He asserted his willingness to serve if he were ever called upon to do so, derided the hysteria that supposed he was shirking when in fact he had not been accepted, and asserted his conviction that his present efforts to serve his country—he had nearly killed himself with the active part he had played in the Defence Loan Campaign—together with his film work, was of more value to the community than his presence in the trenches as a Tommy of poor physique.

He also pointed out sardonically that he could, had he wished, have enjoyed a vast amount of publicity at the time he had volunteered, but, he said with dignity, "All that I have done, all that I am doing, all that I intend to do, to prove my devotion to the cause of democracy, had not been and will not be publicly exploited."

As a result of this statement, letters poured in from all over the world, assuring him of the value of his work, both in the studio, and on the platform at the exhausting public meetings where he helped to raise enormous sums of money for the war effort. There was a universal demand that he be left in peace; and, in effect, he was never called up.

It was his first experience of press persecution, and he was appalled and angered by it. There was nothing then to tell him that it would be his portion for the rest of his life, growing more violent and more widespread as the years went by.

Suddenly and unexpectedly, in September, 1917, Chaplin married Mildred Harris, a fifteen year old film extra. Chaplin, volatile, emotional, and with an inward loneliness that nothing could assuage, was always immediately attracted by beautiful young women. Mildred Harris was very young and very beautiful, with shining golden hair and candid blue eyes, and Chaplin was immediately captured by her. But not even his intimates, not even his brother Syd, had realized that his infatuation was more than a momentary worship of the beauty he could never resist.

They had watched, with amusement or alarm, as Chaplin the great film star sent flowers daily to the little film extra, invited her to dine with him, and waited for hours in his car outside the studio where she was engaged. Yet in spite of this ardent courtship, his marriage came as a shock to his friends.

The marriage was bound to end in disaster. Chaplin was too subtle and complex a person to be able to live in harmony with a child who had no taste in common with him, no point of character that met his, and an undeveloped mind that could not reach his own. There was the shining golden hair, the wonderful eyes, the youth that had englamoured him, but nothing more. And for her there was the impossibility of understanding and appreciating a personality beyond her experience. They had a child, which died; and in two years, Mrs. Chaplin gave up her struggle, and sued for divorce, which was granted her.

Chaplin, as always, refused to give any information to the press, and endured in silence the calumnies and scurrilities that were published. Miss Harris tried vainly to explain why she found it impossible to live with Chaplin, and earned pity in some quarters, and condemnation as a little gold digger in others. Whatever may have been her reason for entering into the marriage, her statements to her lawyers and the press reveal the incompatibility between her husband and herself.

She told how Chaplin would leave her alone for hours on end, while he went down to the beach and stared moodily at the sea, never moving; how he would seem sometimes not to be aware of her at all, not answering when she spoke. Or he would turn to music for hours at a stretch, utterly absorbed, while she sat by, ignored and unwanted. He was always charming and kind when she was ill, but never concerned about her reactions to the times he absented himself for days on end, without warning, without explanation; or the effect upon her nerves of his silence and his withdrawal into his own melancholy.

All this is evidence of an unbridgeable chasm, with suffering on both sides. Mildred Harris married Cinderella's Prince, only to have him transformed into a moody creative genius beyond her ken, while Chaplin married a dream, and found nothing when he woke. He was too absorbed in his work, too caught up with the processes of his creative impulse, to be even aware that his wife was in fact a real person requiring rather more attention than he gave her, and young enough to be eager for amusement.

There is an ironic revelation of the gulf between them in an incident that took place when Chaplin accompanied Sam Goldwyn to a Los Angeles hospital to see a friend, some time after the divorce.

Chaplin wandered about on his own while Goldwyn was with his friend, and found his way into a little sitting room. It contained a vast number of books, all obviously belonging to someone who enjoyed poetry, novels and literary criticism of the highest intellectual order, and Chaplin examined them with interest. A nurse came enquiringly towards him, obviously not recognizing him.

"Whose room is this?" said Chaplin.

"This? Oh, it's being used by Mrs. Mildred Harris Chaplin. Those are her books."

"So this is what she reads."

"Oh, no. The books she *reads* are in the locker in her bedroom." And they both laughed, for very different reasons.

Chaplin was forced henceforward to live his private life, to a very large extent, in the public eye. And his public life was also everybody's business. Everyone, from society women to young film extras, who wanted a successful career in films laid siege to him, and many went to the most extravagant lengths to secure publicity, or an engagement, through him.

There was one who arranged her own kidnapping in an attempt to bring herself more firmly to Chaplin's notice; there were others who fought to be photographed with him, who inserted notices in the press coupling his name with theirs. Chaplin began to feel like an unwilling Haroun al Raschid. His whole life was lived henceforward under the unremitting glare of constant publicity; and that part of the price he had to pay for his celebrity irked him considerably. He had accepted, as part of his position, the demands of normal publicity. But the excessive prying into his everyday concerns, the impossibility of achieving for more than a few moments either privacy or solitude, both of which he had always needed, were a heavy and unexpected cross to bear.

But, however unpleasant the incessant demands of would-be film stars, hangers-on and socialites, however wearisome the constant publicity, whatever his private tragedy, Chaplin could always turn with relief to his work. Once he had started a film, his absorption in it was so complete that he was unaware of anything outside its orbit.

Some time after his divorce, he was busily engaged upon *The Kid*, one of the best-remembered of his early films, and one which made a star overnight of a little boy of seven.

✍ The Wonderful Visit

THOUGH ALL THE SUBSTANCE OF CHAPLIN'S FILMS, AS WE SHALL SEE later, is subjective, and much of its incident drawn from his own experiences, *The Kid* stands alone in that it is as autobiographical as *David Copperfield* was for Dickens.

His own poverty-stricken childhood, his need of his mother, his desolation when he was snatched from her, the background of want and insecurity he had lived through were reproduced in the film, and shared between Charlie and his adopted waif.

Chaplin loved children, as all emotional and sensitive men do, but they terrified him. Their directness, their simplicity, above all their assurance, made him feel conscious of his shortcomings; and he found it difficult to talk naturally and simply to them.

But Chaplin's relationship with Jackie Coogan, the child of the film, was one of the happiest and most successful of his life. He made the small boy into an artist as he had made Edna Purviance into an artist, with infinite patience and tenderness and tact, and an exact knowledge of the end he had in view.

Charlie's tremendous protective love of *The Kid* in the film was based on the truth of Chaplin's love for the child in real life; and Jackie Coogan adored the man who took him into the fantastic world of film.

There was a moment when Chaplin was directing Jackie in one of the most pathetic incidents in the film—the scene in which he is torn from Charlie's arms when they are hiding from the officials who are seeking them out. Jackie had astounding dramatic talent, and his real life relationship with Chaplin lent such poignancy to the scene as Jackie rehearsed it that suddenly Chaplin pushed the child into his father's arms,—"You'll have to take over! I simply can't stand it! I can't stand it!"

And Coogan senior was astounded to see that Chaplin was himself almost in tears, cursing and muttering to ward off the breakdown the child had provoked in him.

When *The Kid* was released, it was hailed throughout the world as Chaplin's finest film; and it is still regarded as one of the best he ever made. It was universally successful. Yet, when it was just finished, Chaplin himself was utterly despondent about it, and fearful of the reaction of the critics. In this mood of discouragement, he asked Sam Goldwyn to come and see it, and advise him on its improvement. Sam, who profoundly admired Chaplin's work, went that very day. Even he was not prepared for the impact of the film, and the enormous progress made since *A Dog's Life*, *Shoulder Arms* and *Sunnyside*, the outstanding films previously made for First National.

As Goldwyn roared with laughter, wiped away a surreptitious tear, moved in his seat in ecstatic delight, or remained still in moments of deep emotion, Chaplin watched his reactions with incredulous eyes, in which a faint hope dawned.

When the lights went up again, Goldwyn was silent, while poor Charlie fidgeted beside him and grew sick with despair. "Charlie—if this is the last picture you were ever destined to make, you'd go down into history with it."

"Gosh!—You're not just cheering me up? You do honestly think it's good?"

"Listen—what you've got is a bad attack of movie blues! Try it out on some others. I'll give a dinner over at my studio, and we'll show it afterwards."

"Maybe. But if you're going through with it, you'd better see it's a good dinner—they'll need it!"

Goldwyn never has done things by halves. Among those invited to his banquet on this occasion were Somerset Maugham, Edward Knoblock, Elinor Glyn, Rupert Hughes, Rex Beach, Elsie Ferguson, Pauline Frederick and Sir Gilbert Parker.

As the film wound its length, Chaplin, petrified with mingled terror and timidity, sat huddled on the fringe of the crowd. But of all the private previews Goldwyn had either given or attended, there had never before been one like this. Chaplin nearly disappeared beneath the onslaught. Every woman present wanted to kiss him, every man slapped him on his aching back, and never before in his wholly successful film career had he been complimented so sincerely in such glowing terms. All the women had wept, and some of the men. Chaplin, bathed in their tears, warmed by their kisses, shattered by their backslapping and their almost frantic admiration and excitement, turned pale and giddy.

It was Elinor Glyn who released the tension. Soulfully she said, in her grandest manner, "This is the finest film I have ever seen in my life!"

"Have you seen many?"

"Well—no. This is my first."

Once *The Kid* was well launched on its meteoric career, and Chaplin's misgivings about it set at rest, he began work on his next film, *The Idle Class*, finished it in record time, and started another immediately. The sets were built, the actors engaged and in attendance for a big scene, made up and in costume. A hundred extras were dressed and ready, in addition. At that moment, Chaplin decided to go to Europe, in spite of the waiting crowd, and the four months' work already put in on the film. Nothing could move him from his decision —persuasion, cajolery, anger, the thought of wastage. He blandly announced that he was going; and went. Apparently "A steak and kidney pie, influenza and a cablegram were the triple alliance that is responsible for the whole thing," in the words that opened his lively book, *My Wonderful Visit*, the book he afterwards wrote concerning this first trip to Europe since he became famous.

Having started the film, he had found himself tired, ill, and depressed after a bout of influenza. In this mood, he accepted an invitation to dine at the home of Montagu Glass, who enticed him with steak and kidney pie; and the homely dinner party roused nostalgia, and made him restless. On his return, a cablegram from London was waiting for him, urging him to attend the première of *The Kid*, and suddenly he made up his mind to go. It seemed the answer to everything that was troubling him; and he had never yet attended a première of one of his films outside America.

His excitement as his boat docked at Southampton was enormous, and tinged with uncertainty and apprehension—he did not know how he would be received, after so long. He was used to being enthusiastically mobbed whenever he made a public appearance in the States. But this was his own country, and he the young Cockney lad returning after many years.

Nothing prepared him for the great reception he received in London; he was almost overborne by a mob that struggled and fought to reach him, that shouted blessings and messages of love and affection, that welcomed him as their own, returned at last, and greatly loved. He was moved to terror, and to a pleasure so intense that he could not contain it, but, catching excitement from the crowd, he began to throw down among them the flowers clustering everywhere in his rooms at the Ritz. In a moment, the police came to beg him not to, for fear of accidents, the crowd was so congested and so determined to get one of these souvenirs.

Mixed with his delight in such evidence of popularity was shame that he should have done so little to deserve it, and a desire to escape from it for a while.

It is typical of him that the very first thing he did after his arrival was to creep out by the back way and to go straight to Kennington, on a solitary pilgrimage that covered all the haunts of his youth. It made an extraordinary impression upon him. Part of him went out to the old familiar things; part shuddered in horror away from the memory of them. Above all, he realized that he had gone too far away in time and in condition ever to get back, however much he desired it, however hard he tried.

"Almost every step brought back memories, most of them of a tender sort. I was right here in the midst of my youth, but somehow I seemed apart from it. I felt as though I was viewing it under a glass.

It could be seen all too plainly, but when I reached to touch it it was not there—only the glass could be felt, this glass that had been glazed by the years since I left. If I could only get through the glass, and touch the real live thing that called me back to London. But I couldn't."

Later, he took some of his friends to one or two of the haunts of his childhood, including one of the dingy attics where once he had lived with Syd and his mother. Worm-eaten stairs with a creaking greasy banister led to a small dark room lit by an oil lamp and furnished with the barest necessities. Crumbling walls, a sullen fire on the small hearth, an indescribable atmosphere of poverty and want struck them all into silence while Chaplin, with trembling lips and tear-filled eyes, stared into the past. Almost immediately, with a sudden change of mood, he was looking for the hole in the floor through which he and Syd in turns watched the woman below undressing. He chatted for a while with the present tenant, a bed-ridden old lady, and when they all left, he made a pretext for returning, and slipped some money into her hand, knowing to the last farthing what it would mean to her; so small a sum now to the boy from Kennington; such unimaginable wealth to the old lady who lived there still.

At the other end of the scale was as fantastic a social life. Chaplin discovered that he was the most sought-after man in London, with an entrée to the most distinguished houses, a welcome guest, accepted on equal terms with the greatest personalities of the time in literature, politics, art and society. It was on this visit that he began one of his rare lasting friendships—with Sir Philip Sassoon. It was a real relationship of a kind that have been few indeed in Chaplin's life.

He met, in the course of his visit, E. V. Lucas, J. M. Barrie, Squire Bancroft, Bruce Bairnsfather, Thomas Burke, H. G. Wells, Gerald du Maurier, St. John Ervine and Lady Astor, and was royally entertained by them.

It was an exhausting and enthralling visit. On the one hand, the nostalgia of the past, on the other the continuous social engagements; throughout, the solid evidence of astonishing fame and popularity. His fan mail was so enormous that numerous secretaries were called in to deal with it. In the first three days of his visit he received seventy-three thousand letters and cards; over a third of them were begging letters. And he discovered from them that he had nearly seven hundred relatives in London that he knew nothing about, nine of whom claimed to be his mother.

He was entirely captured by the charms of The Albany, where Knoblock had an apartment. The dignity and grandeur of the old building, its historic associations, impressed him, as did Knoblock's apartment itself. But his genuine appreciation did not prevent him from carrying out, in that setting, an elaborate joke on Tom Geraghty, formerly Douglas Fairbanks' scenario writer, at this time a free-lance, and one of Chaplin's oldest friends.

There was a small crowd in Knoblock's apartment one night, and gradually conversation turned on Chaplin. Nearly all present agreed that he was really at the apex of his career, and that the London visit proved it. Tom Geraghty, with simple sincerity, suggested that the only thing to do, when such a peak was reached, was to die, since anything afterwards was bound to be an anti-climax and therefore inartistic.

Outside, a thunderstorm was raging, with sheets of lightning flashing across the dark sky; and together, Chaplin and Knoblock began to build an eerie atmosphere of tension and dread, helped by the gale rattling the window frames, the storm without, and a preoccupation with death, violence and the inexplicable force of nature in their conversation. Suddenly, a great flash of lightning turned every face livid, etched in the dark shadows of cupboard and corner. Chaplin, jerked suddenly to his feet as though by invisible forces, let out an eldritch shriek, grew rigid and fell upon his face.

There was a frightening silence, then confusion. Someone telephoned for a doctor, others carried the stiffened body into an adjoining bedroom, while Tom Geraghty was petrified with shock, and then overcome with anxiety. No one paid any attention to him, everyone rushed busily round, summoning a coroner, getting into touch with the police, while Geraghty's panic grew.

When Chaplin, enfolded in the sheet, with pillowcases for wings, floated into the room as an angel, Geraghty's panic turned to furious anger.

"It's blasphemy, that's what it is, blasphemy! Blaspheming death!" he roared. Never were angel's wings so securely clipped: and henceforward, in the circle of Chaplin's friends, that incident was referred to as the blaspheming death.

The same impulse that had taken Chaplin, without warning, across the Atlantic, took him as suddenly to Paris. Here, Chaplin found himself spiritually at home. The quicker tempo of living, the whole vibrant atmosphere of the lovely city answered something in him, and he was at once at ease. His French name—Charlot—pleased him enormously, and he signed it with elaborate flourishes whenever autograph-hunters approached him.

His fame and popularity in Paris were as great as in London, and his entry into the city was a repeat performance of his entry into London. His old friend Cami, the cartoonist, was there to greet him.

The two artistes had corresponded for years, exchanging sketches and photographs. But this was the first time they had ever met, and their meeting was complicated by the fact that Chaplin spoke no French, Cami no English.

With Waldo Frank, Dudley Malone, and others, he went to the *Lapin Agile* and there enjoyed what he called "an evening of rareness"—due mainly to the haunting beauty of the playing of the violinist René Chedecal, and the atmosphere of intelligent creative power that was wrapped around the place.

After the exhilaration of Paris and his reception there, his visit to Germany was at first disappointing—for his films had not reached that country and he was unknown there—and later compensated for by his meeting with Pola Negri at the Palais Heinroth, Berlin's most exclusive and expensive night club of the period. They were immediately attracted to each other. If Mildred Harris had been typical of one kind of woman whom Chaplin always found attractive, Pola Negri represented to the highest degree the other type of woman he was always drawn towards.

She was a Pole, extremely beautiful in a subtle and exotic way, a sophisticated and experienced woman of the world. From their first meeting, they were inseparable; and what had seemed at first the least exciting part of his European tour was transformed by her advent. She opened for him the great houses of Berlin, and he achieved the social distinction he had already enjoyed in London and Paris.

On one occasion, he was present with her at a formal dinner in one of the great baroque palaces abounding. His total ignorance of German forced him into so many gaffes—as when he joined in the toast to himself, or toasted the wrong bride-to-be that, by the time he was called upon to make a speech he had lost his nerve.

He rose to his feet, a very small man at a very large banquet, licking dry lips, and praying for speedy death. Suddenly, he caught sight of Pola Negri further down the vast table, her large dark eyes fixed upon him in understanding and amusement, her mouth curved in the slightest smile. As though she had opened the way for him, he began to mime his speech. Not a single word came from him; there was a profound silence in the vast hall, until, at a signal from him, the Russian musicians launched themselves into wildest Cossack music. Chaplin, bringing his mimed speech to its silent peroration, left his seat and danced. He danced to his hostess, his host, the betrothed couple for whom the dinner was given, and finished his dance on his knees before Pola Negri, kissing her outstretched hand. Sober Teutons shouted and clapped and yelled for more; a society famous for its rigidly conventional behaviour, its unbreakable shibboleths, took to its suddenly illuminated bosom the little man who had made, through mime and dancing, the most eloquent and brilliant after-dinner speech they had ever heard.

Exhausted, stimulated and deeply satisfied, Chaplin, after a few days more in Paris and a hasty farewell visit to London, set out for home. He had made his conquest of Europe, recovered from his period of depression, and left behind notable friends who would gladly welcome him again with the same fervour whenever he returned to Europe.

It was hard to leave Pola Negri. Later, when she announced her intention of taking up film work in Hollywood, he was able to arrange considerable advance publicity for her, which helped her in her rapid rise to fame on the American screen. When she came, they were once more inseparable, reputed engaged, said to have parted, reputed engaged again, finally going their separate ways.

As soon as Chaplin set foot on American soil again, he was besieged with magnificent offers to write an autobiographical narrative of his visit. Chaplin the canny business man accepted the best offer, and dictated the forty-thousand word book on his train journey across America. His enthusiasm and excitement were so intense that the book was finished by the time the train reached Salt Lake City. Chaplin was paid twenty-five thousand dollars for *My Wonderful Visit*, a sum which helped considerably to defray the expenses of the trip.

The book is well worth reading for its revelation of Chaplin's personality, his artist's reaction to the people he met, the adventures he had, and the effects of returning to his own land as the most famous celebrity of his time.

The day of his return from Europe, he dashed straight to Goldwyn's office, and plunged into a vivid description of his triumphal tour. Goldwyn sat back comfortably to witness a one-man show of no mean order, while Chaplin acted and mimed the whole tour for his benefit, playing all parts, assuming all nationalities, using all voices, and re-creating, in a Hollywood office, the total impact of his Wonderful Visit.

✍ Public Success and Private Disaster

FOR SOME TIME AFTER HIS RETURN HE WAS RESTLESS, UNABLE TO settle, and enduring what one of his secretaries called "the incubating period", when he was seeking and rejecting ideas, then brooding over the one that appealed to him as the theme for his next film—in this case *The Pilgrim*, the last film he was to make for the First National Company.

The film was largely directed against Anglo-American puritanism, always a source of fecund satire for Chaplin, and particularly so in this case since his divorce from Mildred Harris had unleashed a flood of scurrilous stories concerning him, which had even extended to the recent arrival of his mother in California.

Though Chaplin's early and close devotion to his mother had naturally been changed through his long-continued absence from England, he had never failed to surround her with every luxury his now comfortably large purse could buy, to make up for the lean and terrible years of his boyhood, when she had nearly died under the struggle. When he decided, for the sake of her health, to bring her to California, he was subjected to more of the calumny he had grown to expect from certain sections of the press.

It was said that he had refused to pay the expenses of her journey, so that she had been obliged to travel steerage. She was, therefore, so it was reported, interned on Ellis Island and refused admission to America, being without visible means of support. And it was only upon the intervention of a lawyer that her unworthy son, against his will, sent just enough money to release her.

The facts were exactly opposite. Hannah Chaplin had travelled luxuriously, with a nurse and a companion in constant attendance. Her meeting with her son was made more moving because she did not realize at all he was a world-famous figure; and to the day of her death she did not know of his world-conquest.

He had bought for her a beautiful house at Santa Monica, facing the sea, and there installed her with her nurse and companion, and every luxury and comfort an invalid could desire or need. He was adversely criticised when these facts were made known, because he continued to live in his own house, while Syd occupied one beside the studio on La Brea Avenue. The press clearly felt cheated of a charming family picture.

Chaplin suffered acutely under this barrage, which overwhelmed him at a time of anxiety and preoccupation. He was intensely worried about his mother's health, since it was clear that she was failing. At the same time he was absorbed in plans to establish the United Artists Corporation, an independent company he intended to form with his old friends Mary Pickford, Douglas Fairbanks and D. W. Griffiths. This was his final effort to secure absolute independence in his work, as in that of those who were associated with him. Some part of the originality of his film work has been due to his foresight in securing total independence before the American film industry turned into a vast factory.

His anxieties, domestic and business, were relieved by the arrival in

Hollywood of Peggy Hopkins Joyce, a dynamic personality with the sophistication and chic of Pola Negri, but without her subtlety. During their short and tempestuous friendship, Peggy told Chaplin her life story, at a moment when he was looking for a theme for his first United Artists film.

He had long wished to make a serious film; and his increasing belief in the powers of Edna Purviance, who through all the vicissitudes of his private and public life, had remained beside him, made him want to use her as star in it. Gradually was evolved the idea of a film about a brilliant woman of the world; and soon Chaplin was feverishly at work on *A Woman of Paris*, which was to some degree the cinematic interpretation of incidents in the life of Peggy Hopkins Joyce.

When the film was released in 1923, it was at once censored in fifteen states of America, and met with more adverse criticism than any other of his films had ever achieved. Its pessimism was a shock to a public captured by the comedy and pathos of Charlie the little tramp.

The repercussion of the film upon those who took part in it had an irony of its own. It made Adolphe Menjou, who played the leading male rôle, into a star. It finished the career of Edna Purviance, who was to have been made a star through it.

Adolphe Menjou achieved immediate success with the rôle he played in *A Woman of Paris*, and sustained with minor deviations ever after—the wealthy man-about-town, assured, sophisticated, debonair —at once the quintessence of a type, and the secret dream of millions of women starved of glamour, who had never known sophistication in their own lives. While Edna Purviance sank into obscurity because, as far as her public was concerned, she was profoundly miscast. For them, she had been, since the early Essanay films, the incarnation of beauty and goodness, simplicity and truth, the ideal of womanhood understandably adored by Charlie. They could not accept her as a "fallen woman", in the idiom of the genre.

With this film, the long association between Chaplin and Edna Purviance ended as suddenly as it had begun. He never used her in a film again, and after a few attempts at work in other studios she vanished from the world of cinema, and died some years later in poverty, unhonoured and unsung. Part of her tragedy was that in this film she showed considerable distinction as an actress.

For Chaplin, the film was an artistic rather than a financial success, and added to his reputation as a director of original films. As soon as it was launched, Chaplin turned to a subject that had long since captured his imagination—the Klondyke gold rush. The ideas that for a long time had been simmering now came to the forefront of his

The Man who made the Films

The character he created

Making a Living
(February, 1914)

The New Janitor
(September, 1914)

Dough and Dynamite
(October, 1914)

The Vagabond
(July, 1916)

Easy Street
(January, 1917)

The Cure
(April, 1917)

The Kid (1921)

The Kid (1921)

A Woman of
Paris (1923)

The Gold Rush (1925)

The Gold Rush (1925)

The Love Look. City Lights (1931)

Money a Mixed Blessing. City Lights (1931)

The Saddest Film with the Funniest Gags. The Circus (1925)

mind, and he determined to make the film, even though it proved impossible to make it in Alaska, since the conditions of work there were too difficult.

Now that Chaplin was determined, no obstacle could be allowed to stand in his way, not even the geographical contours of the land. He transported his entire company, executives and apparatus, to the Rocky Mountains, and there re-built the Klondyke. A pathway 2,300 feet long, with an ascent of 1,000 feet was cut, at a height of nearly 10,000 feet, to make the Chilkoot Pass in the Klondyke. That part of the film-making cost £12,000 and the production costs were £200,000. a fabulous sum in the film world of 1924.

For his leading lady in this film, to be called *The Gold Rush,* Chaplin had chosen an extremely beautiful sixteen-year-old, Lolita Mac-Murray. A few years before, she had been one of the child angels in the dream sequence of *The Kid;* then Chaplin, looking round for his lead in the Klondyke film, noticed her again, fell in love with her, gave her a screen test, and offered her the lead. As Lita Grey, she signed the contract.

Once that part of the business was concluded, Mrs. MacMurray practically assumed possession of the studio. A dominant, aggressive woman, with her daughter's material interests very much at heart, she very cleverly manipulated Chaplin's heartwhole infatuation until the whole company, much against its will, revolved round the untried sixteen year old star.

The combination of extreme youth and extreme beauty proving, as always, irresistible to Chaplin, and the girl's mother insistent, Chaplin married Lita Grey soon after *The Gold Rush* was begun.

Almost immediately, he discovered that he had acquired a militant mother-in-law determined to rule her daughter, her daughter's husband, his public, private and artistic life. She failed only where his work was concerned; in all else life became rapidly intolerable. Once more Chaplin had acquired a very young wife with whom he had nothing in common; and this time, in so doing, he turned his home into a noisy and public guest house. For Lita Grey, with her mother beside her, enjoyed to the full the excitement and gaiety that Mildred Harris yearned for, but did silently without. There can be little doubt that, from the beginning, there was friction between Chaplin and Mrs. MacMurray, and that her influence over her daughter prevented any possibility of a real marriage being established. Lita, young, pleasure-loving, and a born coquette, suddenly set down in a life of luxury and ease, with every hope of a successful film career, plunged into the most hectic social life imaginable, at a time when Chaplin was in the throes of a new film.

One result of this unfortunate marriage was that he was forced to re-make the greater part of the scenes already taken. The two women had not realized soon enough that nothing was ever allowed to come before Chaplin's work. He was determined to keep the predatory hands of wife and mother-in-law away from it, determined that Lita Grey should not use him to make a film career. His decision increased the friction of his domestic life, but gave him freedom in his work, where Georgia Hale replaced Mrs. Chaplin as leading lady.

The Gold Rush, when it was released, was an enormous success, both artistically and financially, and remains one of Chaplin's best loved films.

When *The Gold Rush* was completed, Chaplin himself was for the first time satisfied with a film he had made, and told Goldwyn that this was the film he wished to be remembered by. The critics and the public united to acclaim "Chaplin's hour of sovereign triumph in the picture reels", as one leading authority in America flamboyantly wrote.

In the spring of 1925—the year that saw the release of *The Gold Rush*—Chaplin's son Charles junior was born. This event did nothing to bring husband and wife together; and by the time a second son, Sydney, arrived in 1926, it was clear that nothing could serve to put the marriage upon a happier footing.

Night after night Chaplin roamed round the suburbs of Hollywood, prey to gloom, and the loneliness that could only be lifted from time to time by few and chosen friends. He was unwilling to spend any time at all in a home where there was neither peace nor rest, a home filled with Lita's gay young crowd, picked up here and there at random, eternally crooning, dancing, jazzing, and chattering against the blaring of phonographs and incessant jangling of the piano. Chaplin had out-grown, had indeed never had, any interest in high school high jinks.

The conflict and unhappiness of his private life at this time is reflected in *The Circus,* the film he made next. In spite of its comedy —and the film contains some of Chaplin's funniest gags—the atmosphere of the film is one of exhaustion and melancholy. The lead in the film was given to Merna Kennedy, a childhood friend of Lita Grey, who afterwards denied that she had secured the part for her friend.

Suddenly, and for what seemed a trivial cause, the whole of the pent-up irritation and hatred accumulated since the beginning of the marriage came to a head, soon after the birth of the second son. Chaplin came home one day from the studio, exhausted and on edge after an arduous day's work, to find the house filled, as usual, with a noisy band of tipsy men and women, laughing and yelling and filling the night with their cacophony.

Chaplin's resistance snapped. There was a monstrous scene, in which, beside himself, he ordered Lita's half-scared guests out of the house. Lita went with her guests, taking the children with her, and filed her petition for divorce immediately.

This time was infinitely worse than the previous occasion, for there had been no malice in Mildred Harris, while there was an accumulated resentment of long standing in Mrs. MacMurray, who had never forgiven Chaplin for making *The Gold Rush* without Lita.

Lita's petition was filled with sensational accusations, all of which were avidly seized upon by that section of the press which had already vilified Chaplin over a period of years.

As before, Chaplin took refuge in silence. He went to stay with his brother Syd, his own house being closed to him since Lita's lawyers had impounded all his property, including the studio, pending the case.

The case was made as unsavoury as it well could be, and Chaplin retreated into the fastnesses of a depression that was all but suicidal. Every circumstance of his private life was made the subject of public and scurrilous discussion, and his enemies tasted all the satisfaction of scourging the man who was down.

He could not lose himself in his work, since he was denied access to his property; he could not escape the full glare of publicity. There is no doubt that this period in his life was the worst he was called upon to endure; and his life had never been easy, or particularly happy.

He saw finally that the dice were loaded too heavily against him, and that there was nothing he could do to combat the campaign that was being levied against him. He went to his old friend and lawyer in New York, Nathan Burke; and while his fate was being settled, he was at last mercifully unconscious of the struggle. His arrival in New York was followed by a total collapse; and only the devotion of Burke, and the unremitting efforts of the doctors he called in, saved Chaplin's life, and his reason.

Lita Grey won her case at a cost to Chaplin of his reputation, his health, and a million dollars. But in due course, Chaplin finished *The Circus*, and that he did so was abundant testimony to his courage and his tenacity. As he had built the Chilkoot Pass in the Rockies, so he achieved the infinitely more difficult task of finishing a film begun at a time of great stress, held up by domestic catastrophe, and completed in circumstances that were all adverse—ill-health, nervous exhaustion and near-ruin. He worked like a man possessed on the film, while none of his associates believed it would be possible for him to force himself to the end.

The success of the film when it was released was balm to the wounding of his pride and his prestige, and financially helped to cover the vast amount he had paid out to Lita Grey. Chaplin himself did not find the film very good; he did not enjoy the feeling of satisfaction that *The Gold Rush* had given him.

His own dissatisfaction with *The Circus* led him to plunge into another film less than a month after its completion, a rare thing for Chaplin, who tended to brood over his themes for increasingly long intervals. It is possible that his personal unhappiness found relief in creative work, in activity. Maybe the total absorption in his work that he always experienced was a panacea to the wounds from which he was still smarting.

Whatever the daemon possessing him, this time Chaplin had plunged into his next film before *The Circus* was released.

✑ The Coming of Talkies

FOR HIS NEXT FILM—"CITY LIGHTS"—CHAPLIN WORKED FOR months with four collaborators, Henry Clive, Crocker, Henry Bergman, and his secretary and press agent, Carl Robinson. At least twenty scripts were drawn up, written and rejected by Chaplin, who was still working like a man possessed. Eventually a script more to his liking than those so far presented made him decide to begin the film, and re-shape the scenario if need be as he worked.

It was at this moment that panic struck Hollywood, and the world of cinema was shaken by revolution. Since 1923, the well-known Warners Brothers' studio had been experimenting with sound synchronization with increasing success. In 1927, with their release of *The Jazz Singer,* starring Al Jolson, the crisis was reached. By the end of 1929, Warner Brothers had brought about so comprehensive a revolution in film technique that the motion picture industry as a whole was forced to accept the innovation or go out of business. The "talkies" were launched. With their advent, many stars of the silent films were plunged into ruin, and forced to find some other means of livelihood. Others took lessons in voice production, elocution, or singing, to fit themselves for the new demands made upon them. Only Chaplin resolutely refused to have anything to do with the innovation.

As early as 1921, on his visit to Europe, Chaplin had discussed the possibility of synchronizing voice with movement. He had met St. John Ervine, while he was spending a week-end with H. G. Wells, and they had talked together at some length, since St. John Ervine was very much interested in the idea. But Chaplin, who was first of all a mime, and sincerely believed that mime was infinitely superior to declamation, had been opposed to the whole idea: "I don't find the voice necessary, it spoils the art as much as painting statuary. I would as soon rouge marble cheeks. Pictures are pantomimic art. We might as well have the stage. There would be nothing left to the imagination."

The intervening years, the growth of general interest in sound synchronization, and the release of talkies, had not caused him to change his mind. For in 1929 he was saying to a *Motion Pictures* reporter, "Talkies? You can say I detest them! They come to ruin the world's most ancient art, the art of pantomime. They annihilate the great beauty of silence."

At a moment then when all other studios in Hollywood were installing new apparatus, studying new technique, and dismissing certain of the stars, Chaplin on La Brea Avenue doggedly went on with the making of a silent film.

Virginia Cherrill was chosen for the lead in this film, largely because, in Chaplin's eyes, she bore a strange resemblance to Edna Purviance. She was short-sighted and, without her spectacles, looked like a blind girl. She had never made a film before or been on the stage; and Chaplin began the task he most enjoyed—that of taking raw living material, and moulding and shaping it into an artist. Edna, Jackie Coogan and now Virginia Cherrill. It seemed as though, after the recent unheavals both in his private and his public life, he had come out into the sun again. His old vitality returned, his absorption in his work. The neurotic disappeared, and in his place the studio found a dynamic and amusing director, who kept them moving until they dropped from exhaustion.

Then, before *City Lights* was more than well begun, he was called upon to face more suffering. His mother had suddenly been taken so ill that she had had to be removed to a nursing home. Her doctors at first had been able to reassure Chaplin, but later it became clear that she would not recover. Chaplin was summoned urgently, and went to the nursing home, where he stayed talking for over an hour with his mother's companion, and her doctor.

When he returned to the car where Carl Robinson was waiting for him, his face was pinched and drawn, and he sat down as though strength had suddenly gone from him. He had decided that he would not go to see his mother, who was in a coma; but would keep untouched his memory of her before her last illness changed her. It was clear to Robinson, who knew him extremely well, that in an understandable revulsion of feeling, he would afterwards despise himself for his decision, and all his life regret that he had not seen her at the end.

Chaplin, torn between opposite desires, allowed himself to be persuaded by Robinson, and went back to the nursing home, where he stayed for two hours beside his mother, who only just realized the presence of her son, who could do nothing any more to make up for the lean years.

Robinson meanwhile uneasily wondered how wise he had been in interfering in so intimate a matter: but when Chaplin returned to the car after his ordeal, he said, "You were right, Carl, I feel much better about it all now. She recognized me, and took my hand, and said, 'My boy,' then she lost consciousness again. How glad I am that I was there for that!"

That night, Chaplin sat with Robinson in a Hollywood restaurant, waiting in a state of extreme nervous tension for the news that would mean release for his mother, and loss for himself. It came in the early hours of the morning.

When he set to work again upon the film, it was with renewed energy, and he was keyed to so high a pitch that his close friends were deeply worried.

For inexplicable reasons, or no reason at all, he dismissed both Clive and Crocker. Through Clive's dismissal, he was forced to retake much of the film, for Clive had taken one of the major rôles—that of the eccentric millionaire.

Then, equally suddenly, he took a violent antipathy to his leading lady, Virginia Cherrill, who was told to take a few days' holiday. Studio gossip suggested that Virginia's loss of favour was due to the fact that Chaplin had renewed his earlier friendship with Georgia Hale, and now wanted her to play the sweet blind flower seller. Unfortunately for these plans, Georgia, however disguised with blonde wigs, could not conceal the fact that she was not a fine enough actress to put over a rôle that was utterly foreign to her.

It was clear that Georgia Hale would never take the part, and Chaplin's worried executives watched him trying to replace Virginia Cherrill by various young women, who seemed to have the quality he was seeking, but proved to have neither technique nor skill when they were tested.

Finally, Virginia, who never knew how narrowly she had escaped the loss of her new status, was recalled, and at last this film of many vicissitudes was finished. When it was completed Chaplin realized that, however unwilling he might be to destroy "Charlie" by putting him into a talkie, there was no reason for denying the film a musical sound track.

The young man who once heard the singing of the spheres in a street-corner rendering of *The Honeysuckle and the Bee* had developed over the years into a skilled musician. Now, for three months, he laboured to learn the art of composing, so that he could write the music for *City Lights* himself. He became as absorbed in music as he normally was in film-making. He next took lessons in conducting, and himself conducted the orchestra which made the sound track.

Chaplin has always suffered doubts at the completion of any film, nearly always endured the dissatisfaction of the artist with the finished work, the horror of exposing that work to a possibly indifferent or hostile public. With *City Lights* this feeling was heightened by the fact that, at the climax of the triumph of talkies, he was intending to release a silent film. As always Sam Goldwyn received Chaplin's confession of dread—"You know, Sam, I've spent every penny I possess on *City Lights*. That first showing nearly killed me—it was an absolute Calvary. They're trying to force me to speak. But I will not. I will not! If *City Lights* is a failure, I believe it will strike a deeper blow than anything else that has ever happened to me in this life."

Sam, as always, understood and found the right consolation, and Sam was proved right again.

At the première in Los Angeles in March, 1931, a crowd of 25,000 people surged round the approaches to the cinema in order to see all Hollywood arrive. Large police forces had been mobilized to control the crowd. The whole cinema was floodlit, and the arrival of the stars was announced through loud speakers. At midnight, when the show was over, the crowd was still there, shouting itself hoarse, and yelling for Chaplin.

In London, similar scenes took place when it was shown at the Dominion. Hundreds packed into the vestibule, in the hope of catching a glimpse of Charlie, while thousands waited patiently outside in the pouring rain.

Within the building, Chaplin sat between Lady Astor and Bernard Shaw, watching the film that had suffered so many ills. It was balm to Chaplin's sick spirit to realize that his popularity was undiminished, and his work so greatly loved and admired that the public, excited to fever heat with the advent of talkies, would nevertheless receive his latest silent film with even greater excitement.

While he was in London this time, he visited the Hanwell Institution, where he had spent so unhappy a period as a child. The visit made a tremendous impact upon him, for he is, in his own words, "an emotional cuss". As he looked upon the children before him, a clear picture of the little boy Charlie no doubt came to his mind—the boy Charlie who once forfeited his Christmas orange and bag of sweets because, in his childish excitement over Christmas, he had forgotten to make his bed. The sight of the youngsters now in the place of the child he had been, sent him out to buy compensation for them. He bought a cinema projector, a saxophone, sweets, toys, oranges—everything the child Charlie had longed for, everything these children must long for too.

Yet, when the time came for him to go to distribute this largesse on the following day, he was in another world, having tea with Lady Astor, Amy Johnson and Bernard Shaw. Yesterday's emotional crisis was over, appeased by the gifts he had bought. He refused to leave his tea party. The crowds that had gathered along the road to watch him pass, the children and the staff of the home, were all bitterly disappointed. But Chaplin, yesterday shaken with compassion, haunted by memory, pale and sombre at the thought of children condemned to institutional care, was to-day on top of the world, amusing his fellow guests with a story of how, while he was at work on *City Lights* he had made Douglas Fairbanks eat dust. Douglas Fairbanks, who will be remembered for his picaresque and athletic rôles in *The Black Pirate*, *The Three Musketeers*, *Robin Hood* and the like, was in fact one of Hollywood's finest athletes, and prided himself on keeping fit. Finding Chaplin one morning in a black mood, he first lectured him on his liver, then advised him to take up the cult of physical fitness, and finally challenged him to an early morning sprint the following day from their adjoining homes in Beverley Hills to the studio on La Brea Avenue. Chaplin, roused from his gloom in spite of himself through Fairbanks' exuberant personality, looked solemnly at their reflection in a mirror—Fairbanks tall, bronzed, broadshouldered, and himself, slight, pale, and more than a head shorter. He accepted the challenge, and seemed to wilt under it. The news leaked out, as news will, and next morning the marathon began, to the mingled jeers and cheers of most of the film colony assembled to watch the start. Fairbanks' magnificent torso earned him a round of applause; Chaplin received sympathetic groans.

Fairbanks took the lead; but at the studio gates they were level; and while Fairbanks, panting and exhausted, dropped into a chair, Charlie, showing no sign of strain or stress, sprinted several times round the studio in best professional style, and drew up before his amazed and wide-eyed friend, still pumping his legs vigorously up and down. He then lectured Fairbanks on his liver, advised him to take up the cult of physical fitness and, towelling himself vigorously with Fairbanks' scarf, said laconically—"Kennington Wonder, that's me. Best amateur long distance champion this side of the Cut—but you wouldn't know about that!"

In Berlin, he was mobbed for the first time in that country. His visit to Germany ten years before had been disappointing, since his films were unknown, and himself unrecognized. This second visit showed clearly that in the intervening years Chaplin's popularity had reached the same peak it had attained in England and France and America. In Berlin, he fell in love with Nefertiti; and for years the statue he bought of her stood in his home, and possibly still does.

In Paris, he was nearly torn to pieces by a crowd that had waited day and night to see him arrive. His fame and his popularity had been sustained for ten years upon the incredible peak he had discovered in 1921. In 1931, with *City Lights,* he conquered the world again.

It is fitting that Chaplin should supply the swansong of silent film, an art that was extinguished in full bloom. As *A Woman of Paris* was a milestone in the history of the cinema because it inaugurated a new genre, so *City Lights* was another, in that it marked the end of an epoch in the cinema.

The Humanist in Society

FIVE YEARS ELAPSED BETWEEN THE RELEASE OF "CITY LIGHTS" (1931) and that of Chaplin's next film, *Modern Times* (1936).

His second visit to Europe in 1931 compensated for the troubled early years of his work with United Artists. It was made abundantly clear to him, everywhere in Europe, that his popularity had not suffered through his sensational divorce, nor through the sudden boom of talkies. Unbounded enthusiasm, adulation, worship and, still more important, genuine affection for "Good old Charlie!" or "Ce cher Charlot!" helped to heal the sickness of spirit he had endured since the *Gold Rush.*

His mercurial spirits soared, and he gave himself up to a prolonged holiday on the Côte d'Azur, in Biarritz, as far afield as Algeria, and then in St. Moritz. One or two chosen friends shared the holiday with him, and none more closely than the young May Reeves, an Austro-Hungarian girl who had joined the Chaplin entourage in Paris to help with the international fan-mail that was pouring in from all quarters. May Reeves, who was at home in six languages, was invaluable to a harassed staff, until Chaplin's eye was taken by her unusual beauty. As so many times before, Syd Chaplin and Carl Robinson watched anxiously, dreading the next entanglement, marriage or scandal that might develop.

May Reeves, swept off her feet by the impetuous Chaplin, found herself suddenly launched into an unending social whirl, for Chaplin was pursuing his vacation with the same energy and dynamism that marked his film work. She found him an enchanting and difficult companion. On their first meeting, he suddenly began to dance with her, then by himself—a pas seul as exquisite as anything she had ever seen. His immense zest attracted her, but, like his young wives, she feared and dreaded his sudden descent into gloom, his silence, his complete withdrawal from his friends and colleagues into a world of his own, to which she had no key.

As they enjoyed that extended holiday together with a nucleus of faithful souls who stayed always, and others who were suddenly dismissed, or fell by the way for reasons of their own, she had frequent cause to wonder at his powers of entertainment.

On one occasion, following a luncheon party in the South of France, he acted a French divertissement, in which he played the three rôles —wife, husband, lover—apparently speaking a fluent and colloquial French, so that all save French-speaking people present were amazed at his command of the language. He followed this with scenes from Japanese plays—a form of theatre he seriously admired, insisting that the Japanese trained in the traditional forms were the finest actors in the world. He introduced this sketch in what appeared to be Japanese; and it was only later that his guests realized he had no knowledge either of French or Japanese. It is interesting, in view of this spontaneous clowning in his private life, to remember that in the film he was to make on his return—*Modern Times*—there is the amusing sequence of Charlie the waiter, who is forced to take the place of an absent cabaret turn. Charlie gives a patter song in gibberish that sounds extremely gallic.

Much to the relief of his closest friends, May Reeves left the party at St. Moritz; or perhaps it would be truer to say that Chaplin left her there, and set out on the world tour he had suddenly decided to make. He travelled to Japan, where he intended to absorb all that he could of the traditional Japanese theatre, so near in technique to his own work. News of him came from Tokio, Singapore, Egypt: and he did not return to Hollywood until May, 1932, having been away for over a year.

Soon after his return, gossip began to couple his name with that of Paulette Goddard, a beautiful girl of nineteen, described by the columnists as "belonging to the most exclusive set in American society". Chaplin had first met her in California while she was staying in the country house of friends of her family; and very soon they were making frequent visits to Palm Beach and along the coast together.

There is no doubt that Paulette Goddard, more than a little bored with the pleasure round of her normal life, welcomed the distraction provided by Chaplin's difference from any man she had previously met: and her young vanity was fed by the ardent pursuit of one of the most famous men in the world. Chaplin, as always, had found her classic beauty irresistible, and then was delighted by her intelligence and her witty malice. She was as young and lovely as Mildred Harris and Lita Grey had been: but already, at nineteen, she had her share of the sophistication of Pola Negri. Robert Florey's description of her as "la trépidante et délicieuse Paulette" is very apt.

Shortly after their first meeting, they set out together on a cruise of the South Seas. It was during this period that they were secretly married at sea, on June 1st, 1933. It is not very clear why the marriage was kept secret, but certainly as late as April, 1936, Paulette Goddard was referred to as Chaplin's fiancée.

As soon as Chaplin returned to Hollywood after his romantic interlude, the gossips were busy speculating over his next film. All were agreed that Paulette Goddard would be the central figure in it. Her patrician beauty was exceptionally photogenic, and she was eager to enter films. It was certain that Chaplin would enjoy making her into an artist; and he found for her the ideal rôle in the girl waif of *Modern Times*. Here was no forlorn orphan, but a piquant gamine in rebellion against the conditions that had created her outcast state, a foil to Charlie, and his complement.

Modern Times is in effect the meeting place of Chaplin's past torment and present felicity. Storm and strife had matured him, and brought to a head his feeling for the under-dog and the dispossessed: it had crystallized his hatred and contempt for what he had always believed to be the greatest evil of our times—the industrialization of the people. On the other hand, he came to the making of this film after a long period of rest and relaxation, and at the beginning of a marriage that was, in its first years, rapturously happy. These factors gave the film its overtones of radiant good humour. However serious its satire, *Modern Times* glows with a joyousness that radiates from every scene. The film bore every sign of Chaplin's maturity. It was an ironic indictment of the slavery of the machine, and a defence of individuality. It was also Chaplin's happiest film.

One immediate result of the release of *Modern Times* was to add another group to the list of Chaplin's persecutors. A whole section of American society had risen against him for moral reasons, because of his two marriages with young girls, and the subsequent "scandalous" divorces from them: and because of the constant stream of women whose names were associated with his. Another and conservative section were suspicious of his political convictions, claiming to see in his public statements and in his films an open avowal of communist sympathies, or worse. Following *Modern Times*, the moralists and the politicians were joined by the American industrialists, who maintained the system Chaplin derided and satirized in the film.

The outcry against him was now gathering force and momentum; and his own increasingly intransigent attitude added fuel to the fires raging around him. Chaplin the comedian was fast yielding place to Chaplin the humanist. And the latter was deeply concerned with the evils arising from man's inhumanity to man. His next film, *The Great Dictator*, released at the end of the first year of Europe's war against Fascism, in 1940, was a sequel to the film in which he condemned modern social conditions. All his life he had been furiously roused by anything that served to destroy individual force. Hitler was the incarnation of that destructive impulse. Chaplin, therefore, took all the well-known doctrines of dictatorship, and with sublime comedy, exposed their pretentiousness and their sham. So much ill-advised comment was made upon Chaplin's propagandist purposes in making the film that, as so often before, he was forced into a statement:

"Some people have suggested that I made this picture for propaganda purposes. This is far from the truth. I am not interested in propaganda as such—most propaganda is didactic and dull. I made *The Great Dictator* because I hate dictators and because I want people to laugh."

The Great Dictator was Chaplin's first talking film, and the last in which there is any real trace of the Charlie we knew in those far-away days when Hollywood hardly existed, and the little tramp had just begun his long pilgrimage, in the Keystone studios.

The years between the release of *The Great Dictator* (1940) and Chaplin's last film to date, *Monsieur Verdoux* in 1947, were filled with excitements of a dubious kind, that did little to disperse the suspicion and hostility with which Chaplin was regarded in America.

For the third time, his marriage ended in failure. This time it had lasted nine years, and for some of them had been successful. The causes of its slow disintegration were multiple. Paulette Goddard was never as young in spirit as her two predecessors. She had a strong and demanding personality, which developed over the years of fame and wealth and continuous publicity along its own lines.

In her own way, she was as much of an individualist as Chaplin, and as headstrong. For his part, Chaplin had never been known to remain interested for very long in any woman who attracted him. After the rapturous beginning, the clash of personality began, until towards the end of 1941 it was clear that both husband and wife intended to end a marriage that had already ceased to be more than a façade. The name of Burgess Meredith was already being linked with that of Paulette Goddard, while Chaplin was reputed to be interested in the young daughter of Eugene O'Neill.

In 1942, therefore, a divorce took place in Mexico, and Paulette Goddard was granted a divorce settlement of £250,000, largely in jewellery, for which she had an exorbitant passion. She successfully pursued an independent career in films, the only one of his wives to do so.

The repercussions of this divorce were only just dwindling when once more Chaplin found himself in the public eye, and suffering the incurable glare of maximum publicity.

In 1943, he married the eighteen year old daughter of the playwright Eugene O'Neill, much against her father's wishes. There were some who attributed the failure of O'Neill's *The Iceman Cometh* to his concern over his daughter. In the same year, Chaplin was involved in the unsavoury Joan Barry paternity case, in which a young actress sued him as the father of her then unborn child.

The case was taken before the Superior Court of California; and the Hearst press, always among Chaplin's deadliest enemies, began a campaign of abuse that clearly had a political, not a moral, basis. The campaign seemed to have received its impetus from hostility occasioned by speeches Chaplin had made in 1942 in support of the Second Front.

The case dragged on into 1944, by which time Chaplin had been indicted by a Federal Grand Jury in Los Angeles for violation of the Mann Act, on counts of having endeavoured to transport Miss Barry to New York, in order to engage in illicit sexual relations with her; and of conspiring to deprive her of her civil rights.

The case had now taken an ugly turn; for the maximum sentence for these offences were twenty-three years' imprisonment and a fine of nearly seven thousand pounds. Chaplin was acquitted of these more serious charges, but the paternity suit, with a re-trial following disagreement on the first jury, dragged on into 1945, when it was finally decided that Chaplin was the father of the child, now two years old. In the following year, his appeal against the decision was dismissed by the District Court of Appeal in California.

In the witness box, Chaplin suffered at the hands of Miss Barry's counsel, who called him, among other flamboyancies, "a master mechanic in the art of seduction" and accused him of "lying like a cheap Cockney cad"! Chaplin's refusal to apply for American citizenship has long been a grudge against him; and counsel pandered to that grudge.

By the time *Monsieur Verdoux* was released in 1947, Chaplin's own attitude, the recent dramas of his private life, and world events beyond his controlling, had all contributed to arouse his detractors to a point of fanaticism.

Chaplin continued to mould his public and private life according to his own ideas. He expressed those ideas clearly and firmly and would not move from them. He would not become an American citizen, because he did not believe in nationalism. He expressed admiration for the efforts Soviet Russia had made to establish a vigorous home policy, but denied any communist leanings or tendencies, or that he was himself in truth a communist. Over his private affairs he maintained, as always, an unbroken silence. His attitude infuriated the fanatics; and he then presented them with *Monsieur Verdoux*, in which film he reached his peak of subtlety and satire, and in which he excoriated all that his detractors stood for, and were maintained by.

The genesis of *Verdoux* is an interesting one. Orson Welles, whose work comes nearest to Chaplin's in originality and independence, was dining one evening with the Chaplins and, as usual, discussing films. From this discussion came a suggestion that a Welles-Chaplin collaboration on a film concerning the French Bluebeard-murderer Landru, might well make film history. Chaplin found the proposal possible in the mellow after-dinner hours. But by next morning his acumen had reasserted itself; he knew that collaboration between himself and Welles was impossible. Both were essentially independent directors. By now, however, the possibilities of the Landru theme had seized firm hold of his imagination, and he instructed his manager to buy Welles out. That dinner with the Chaplins was a remunerative one for Welles, who gained 25,000 dollars through that half-casual suggestion and presentation of a theme. Landru changed into Verdoux, and his specific pathological homicide was transmuted by Chaplin's alchemy into sociological necessity.

The fate of *Monsieur Verdoux* in America has been interesting. Several powerful groups, led by the Catholic Church, organized so widespread a boycott over the showing of the film that Chaplin was forced to withdraw it from circulation, since managers would no longer book it. In over two years, the film played just over two thousand dates, as compared with the normal showing of twelve thousand dates for the average film.

In Europe, the film achieved a mixed reception. No one denied its quality: Chaplin showed himself to be still a major artist in film. Many praised it highly; but a large proportion of his early public missed Charlie and his ludicrous misadventures, missed the golden humour of the earlier films, and were uneasy over the astringent wit of this one. A few found the film immensely sad, for it seemed that at last Chaplin, creator of the indomitable little tramp Charlie, had given up hope of finding anything at all over the horizon towards which, in the early films, he had shuffled with such unflagging optimism.

Monsieur Verdoux certainly roused increased antagonism in the States. In May, 1947, Republican senator Harry P. Cain (Washington) in a statement to the Senate Judiciary Committee, demanded that Chaplin should be deported, on the grounds that he "almost treasonably" asked Picasso—"a self-admitted French communist"—to head a protest committee in France against the American deportation proceedings against the great German composer and anti-fascist Hans Eisler, which had been organized by the Rankin Committee.

Counterpoise was given to this assessment of Chaplin's value a year later in France by the French Association of Cinema Critics, who proposed unanimously that Chaplin should receive the Nobel Peace Prize, on the grounds that *Modern Times, The Great Dictator* and *Monsieur Verdoux* were outstanding contributions to the better promulgation of peace.

Chaplin stood trapped in a paradox. He enjoyed unparalleled fame and popularity, while at the same time he was the object of unlimited hostility. The same man, much loved and much hated, was a public idol and a public affront. But he went his own way in spite of it all.

The hostility to which Chaplin had been subjected in the United States ever since the last world war, by reactionaries who never relaxed their persecution, reached its climax when he made plans to travel to Europe for the London première of his film *Limelight*. He secured his re-entry permit only after several official interviews and a great deal of difficulty. But he did receive it, and it was therefore a great shock when he was advised by cable, on the journey to Europe, that he would be forbidden re-entry unless he went before an Immigration Board of Inquiry to answer charges of a political nature and of moral turpitude.

This was the virtual end of a love-hate relationship with the U.S.A. that had lasted roughly forty years. Since 1952 he has lived in Switzerland, at Vevey, and his latest film, *A King in New York*, was made in England.

✑ Portrait of a Great Man

MOST PEOPLE ARE SURPRISED WHEN THEY MEET CHAPLIN FACE TO face. Neither the little tramp Charlie of the past, with his wistful eyes, absurd moustache, fantastic walk and ragged finery, nor Verdoux of the present, handsome and elegant man about town, are any preparation for such a meeting.

Time has thickened the outline and silvered the hair of the "slender fellow, smooth shaven, with waves of crisp black hair and dark blue eyes that have the peculiar smoky quality of the autumn hills" whom Sam Goldwyn met over a quarter of a century ago.

His smallness, his feminine hands, and his astonishing eyes are the physical factors that immediately impress those who see him for the first time, together with the mobility of his face, expressing as it does in casual conversations all the facets of his temperament.

He rose from obscurity to meet the blazing sun of international publicity, laudatory and adverse, with a suddenness that might have overthrown him, had it not been for his singleminded absorption in his work. Yet the demands of fame are very great. For him, from the beginning of his career in films, small audiences gave place to the idolatrous worship of the crowd; and he, the poverty-haunted Lambeth lad, earned wealth beyond his wildest dreams. He became, without any volition on his part, a legend, a myth, a name that rang through the world.

It would be difficult for any human being, however assured, to survive such a sudden transformation without some deviations of character. Chaplin was never assured; there was too much insecurity and terror in his background, and he could never escape from the memory of it. Without his artistic integrity, he would have been a lost soul, given over to the worst excesses that his position imposed upon him. Hollywood's reputation as the Babylon of modern times was built by the lost souls who found sudden wealth and fame too much for them, and lost both as quickly as they had been gained.

Chaplin's artistry, and his Cockney shrewdness, saved him in the early years.

His work has brought him enormous rewards and enormous frustrations. He has found release for all time from the cankering fear of poverty that overshadowed his youth. He has earned the freedom to engage upon his work without let or hindrance, his own master always. But fame has robbed him of privacy. He can rarely walk unnoticed through a crowd, never make a film or a statement, a gesture or a mistake, that will not be misunderstood, misinterpreted, magnified or minimised, until it is difficult to apply normal terms of judgment to anything he says or does. In his younger days, demonstrations of popularity—the crowds that followed him, mobbed him, spied upon him, wrote to him—exhausted and terrified him; yet he could not do without the exhilaration of receiving witness of his fame, nor resist playing up to the demands made upon him.

Complex personalities demand great understanding; and for years Chaplin lived in an inward solitude as much forced upon him as sought by him. The morose youth of the Karno days, the taciturn intruder into the Sennett Studios, gave place to the successful young man surrounded by satellites, sycophants, a few real friends, and shoals of aspiring women, whom he alternatively welcomed into rapturous and apparently intimate friendship, and then ignored completely. He was always torn between the desire for human contact and understanding, friendship and love that is common to all mankind; and a far greater desire for absolute liberty. The pattern of his relationships with people has therefore been an erratic one. His immediate and strong reaction to people, his sudden violent friendships, are well-known. So too the fact that he continually thrusts away friends, lovers and colleagues who come too close, in a panic so acute that he will achieve the break by whatever means comes to hand.

The Little Fellow: Latest Aspect
(Limelight, 1952)

Modern Times (1936)

Modern Times (1936)

The Quixotic Boxer. City Lights (1931)

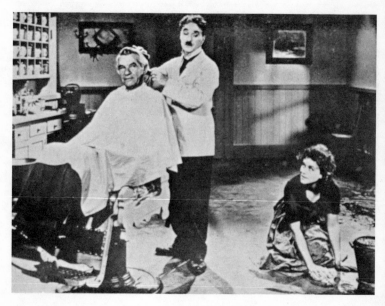

The Jewish Barber. The Great Dictator (1940)

Adenoid Hynkel. The Great Dictator (1940)

Under the Sign of the Double Cross. The Great Dictator (1940)

Modern Times (1936)

The Machine Age

Recognition. Monsieur Verdoux (1947)

The Man about Town. Monsieur Verdoux (1947)

The Cynical Amorist. Monsieur Verdoux (1947)

The Dear Departed. Monsieur Verdoux (1947)

The Connoisseur. Monsieur Verdoux (1947)

Looking Ahead. Monsieur Verdoux (1947)

This double compulsion serves in large measure to explain the accusations of cruelty and ingratitude that have been levelled against him; as it explains the sudden banishment of Edna Purviance after ten years of closest collaboration; of Carl Robinson, who was for sixteen years his confidential secretary; of Cami, devoted disciple from the first time Chaplin ever set foot in Paris. It serves to explain the otherwise inexplicable dismissal of colleagues in the middle of a film; his whole-hearted admirations and aversions; and his determination never to yield to the social or emotional pressure put upon him by those who mistakenly assume that they are indispensable to him.

His great love of power and its exercise may also be a factor in his repudiation of relationships—the quick vivid friendships swiftly ended and forgotten, the wilful destruction of the affection, or passion that he had himself provoked and fostered.

His is a paradoxical character. Everyone who has ever been associated with Chaplin has commented on his capacity for the wildest fooling, his spontaneous and wholehearted gaiety in any assembly, an ebullience of spirits that sweeps the crowd with him whenever he chooses—yet leaves behind it the impression of melancholy held in check.

No one who knows him is surprised when he turns morosely and silently away from the studio, or from a group of friends, suddenly engulfed in a despair that has no issue, a mood of despondency so acute that nothing, not even the exigencies of his work, have been known to lift it until it has run its course.

Quite apart from the loneliness of his youth, largely due to his own maladjustment, his desire for normal social relations has always been complicated by this essential solitude of the spirit, that is inescapable. This isolation is the cause of Chaplin's sadness, that from the beginning was the basis of his clowning. For Chaplin could neither endure nor change the awareness of solitude that had been his all his life, and from which he had never found relief in any companionship or any love affair. Contact with men and women, when it became close, served only to accentuate the hopelessness of any understanding between himself and others. His intelligence was great enough to make him aware of the full implication of his isolation; his sensibility caused him to suffer from it. His courage and his tremendous zest for living have forced him, over the years, to accept the intolerable.

This full acceptance of experience, to which he has always borne witness in his life and in his work, is part of Chaplin's astonishing vigour and positive attitude towards life, his joy and excitement in living.

"I'm an emotional cuss," Chaplin said of himself, and there is a certain ruefulness in the confession. For Chaplin's emotionalism caused him and others much suffering, and set him off on a long search for the ideal woman with an impetuosity that carried him along faster than he could easily travel. His own temperament made him particularly vulnerable to the beauty of women, with the subsequent disillusionment when he found nothing behind the beauty. Chaplin's odyssey of love has, on the whole, contained more suffering than satisfaction.

That extension of his personal solitude, which covers his isolated position in modern American society, the society against which his heaviest guns have been fired in all his films, is understandable.

Always subjective in his thinking, his own passionate desire for freedom puts him always on the side of the under-dog, the downtrodden, the industrial slave; and therefore against the molochs of big business who have robbed mankind of freedom.

His ardour, his vitality, made a crusader of him. His deep sadness, his solitude, were the basis of his desire that all men should have their minimum requirements. It is the basis too of his appeal to humanity as a whole, without frontiers or nations or any limitation of the brotherhood of man. His individuality and his integrity forced him to declare himself on what is, in America, the wrong side—the side of the little man.

Chaplin is a natural anarchist, an individual unit taking a stand on matters of social and political interest according to his own judgment, principles and understanding, regardless of the established order of the society in which he lives. Sometimes he may find himself in line; more often, not, since his own motives, by which he lives, are in almost total opposition to those ruling the society of our times. That is the core of Chaplin's so-called "political" position. Certainly Soviet Russia has extended welcoming arms to him; and his public activities and statements have given rise to an American witch hunt against him for "subversive" tendencies.

A natural anarchist cannot be a communist; the ideologies are at opposite poles, since anarchy gives pride of place to the individual, and communism to the state. Chaplin's natural anarchy leads him to an outlook upon life that is communist in the real, not the party political meaning, of the terms—a desire for the brotherhood of man and for an equal distribution of the world's goods, to secure for each man his basic rights. Being what he is, he finds himself in substantial agreement with the ideals of the social programme of the communist party in Russia; but remote indeed from its practice. He is too much of an individualist, too great an artist, to be able to accept the doctrines of State Socialism.

He is an iconoclast not through any formulated policy—for his thinking, like that of D. H. Lawrence, comes from the heart, not from the head—nor through exhibitionism, but through a total incapacity to fit in with, or accept, the axioms of modern society. Chaplin, like H. G. Wells, wants order, but a New World Order, believes that men are capable of government if they are sufficiently well-intentioned, and receive efficient support from a politically educated mass. In effect, most of the satire of his films, from Keystone days to *Monsieur Verdoux* is directed against the various human frailties and stupidities that prevent the establishment of such order.

Chaplin's political position results from his personality—from his fundamental romanticism with its allied anarchy, that must express itself in its own terms, not as a communist manifesto, but as a declaration of the rights of every man.

Chaplin's whole life has been offensive to the herd mind. The iconoclast is never popular, and Chaplin, because of his intensely personal approach to the problems of living, because of the subjective nature of his work, has been an open target for the fear and malice aroused by his unwavering refusal to yield any part of his individuality.

Together with animosity and hostility, he has enjoyed a world-wide affection that comes rarely to men, and that, in his case, still endures over the greater part of the globe.

To-day, Chaplin, at sixty-three, has lived through the tempestuous years, overcome the strain and suffering, and reached a mellow calm. Behind him stretch the years of hardship, poverty, privation; the years of sudden exciting fame and wealth; the years of personal calamity and struggle and dissatisfaction; the turbulent catastrophes brought about by his own temperament; the years of solitude and sadness and seeking.

His marriage with Oona O'Neill would seem to be the main reason for his present content. Thrice before, his liking for young girls had betrayed him into foolish marriages. Mildred Harris, with her baby doll prettiness, as well as Lita Grey, of the soulful dark eyes, and Paulette Goddard, the ex-Follies girl, had nothing upon which to build a marriage with a mature and complex personality. The eighteen-year-old Oona O'Neill was of quite other stuff. Her reply to the inevitable question of the inevitable reporter, on her wedding day, showed her quality. She was asked why she had chosen as husband a much-married man of scandalous reputation, three times as old as she was. She replied, with a gleam of humour in her intelligent dark eyes, that hers was an esoteric union. The baffled reporter transcribed this perfect reply to press impertinence, and for a long time afterwards everyone explained at great length what she must have meant. The development of her marriage has explained it for her. Contrary to all general expectation, and in spite of the failure of Chaplin's three other marriages, the eighteen year old girl and the fifty-four year old man have achieved, over the years, a vital marriage. Chaplin's own contentment, the atmosphere of his home, prove it.

He has lived for the past twenty years in the same house in Beverley Hills, with its swimming pool shaped like an inverted bowler hat, and its long-treasured bust of the incomparable Nefertiti, with the furnishings and appointments that have scarcely changed over the years. For the little boy who took part in frequent moonlight flits, the youth who lived in dingy rooms on tour, grew into the man who clung to his home, once it was established, through all his marital and other vicissitudes. Even Oona Chaplin must go warily with changes and innovations in the house; but the intelligence that shook the reporter, the intelligence that made her, young though she was, a real companion to her husband, is great enough to secure for her her own way without too much dissent from her conservative partner.

Markova, who first met Chaplin in Hollywood in 1938, soon discovered this conservatism. One hot summer's day, after a gruelling rehearsal, she called in at the Chaplin home, and found a tennis party just finishing. She murmered something about tea, hopefully. Charlie turned eagerly to her—"You've come to the right place. There's a *real* cup of tea going to-day!" And thereupon he led his party into the house to enjoy a "high tea" that was a masterpiece of its kind, and as authentic as any served in London or Lancashire or Yorkshire. Markova was interested to see how, in the midst of Hollywood's extravagant splendour, he lived without ostentation, and remained somehow English to the core.

Part of Chaplin's present content is due to his success as a family man. He and his present wife have four children—Geraldine who is eight, Michael who is six, Josephine who is four, and the one-year-old Victoria. Chaplin's sentimentality, his desire to make up to other children the lacks in his own childhood are satisfied in his dealings with his young family. To the world at large, Chaplin is either the little tramp or America's Big Bad Wolf. To his four children he is a superlative playmate, the most amusing father any family could have.

His relations with his grown-up sons, the children of Lita Grey, have grown close with the passing years. They were handsome children and have become handsome and gifted young men. Charles Chaplin junior, now twenty-seven, and his brother Sydney, who is twenty-six, bear names that are illustrious in the world of film and show signs that they have inherited their father's talents, if not his genius. Charles junior has turned to legitimate theatre, while Sydney will make his screen début in his father's new film *Limelight*.

Two years ago, it was rumoured that the new film was based upon the life of the music-hall star Mark Sheridan, who was very popular in his day. A contemporary of T. E. Dunville, Arthur Reece, and Charles Godfrey, he shared with them the peculiar gusto and vitality of the real music-hall turn. He ended tragically. He shot himself during a breakdown largely due to the belief that the public were growing tired of him. The theme of *Limelight* is that "of an ageing music-hall comedian who wants to make a comeback, but has lost his confidence, and is haunted by the fear that he can no longer get the laughs"—a Chaplinesque transmutation perhaps of Mark Sheridan's tragic suicide.

As work upon the film has progressed, the basic idea has receded into the background, and the theme has developed along other lines. With the second trilogy—*Modern Times, The Great Dictator, Monsieur Verdoux*—Chaplin said all that he had to say about modern society. In the five years since the release of *Monsieur Verdoux*, he has turned back to the London he knew as a child, to the memories of his years in music-hall.

His nostalgia has created the background of his new film, the lost world of English music-hall. Against that background, Chaplin builds the story of Calvaro, the elderly vaudeville comedian attempting a comeback, and stricken with the fear of failure, who falls in love with a young ballerina. She is haunted by the same fear, and her neurosis prevents her from reaching fulfilment as a dancer. Calvaro saves her from suicide, and then forces her to face and conquer her fear, while he himself remains a prey to his own.

In Calvaro, we recognize Charlie the gallant knight, silver-haired now, mature and wise, but still immediately captured by beauty. The Young Girl is still lovely and defenceless, still unattainable. Charlie-Calvaro may succour her in distress, befriend her, restore her life and sanity, release her talent: but her heart, as always, is given elsewhere —to the young composer who loves her.

Enough information concerning the film has been released to arouse interest and curiosity. Into this film of his past, Chaplin has put his posterity. Charles junior is glimpsed in the ballet sequences: Sydney junior plays the young composer, Edgar Neville (the name of a composer who was once one of Chaplin's close friends): while Geraldine, Michael, and Josephine appear as Calvaro's children. Another member of the family to make a brief appearance is Chaplin's half-brother Wheeler Dryden, who plays a doctor.

A factor of interest in the making of this film is that it has led

Chaplin into choreography. Some time ago, Constance Collier (who in the earliest days of her successful stage career herself appeared in music-hall) gave a tea party in her New York flat to reunite old friends. Markova and Dolin were there, on their way back to England. Suddenly the door opened, and Chaplin and his young wife came in, Charlie's eyes vivid with cold, and both glad to escape for a while the freezing temperature outside.

Chaplin, even before he had removed his coat, had begun to tell them of an idea for a ballet—*The Death of Columbine*—he planned to include in his new film. Leaping to his feet, thrusting his cup at Oona, he began to dance and mime the theme, giving so vivid an impression of the whole ballet, in such detail, that Markova and Dolin saw exactly what he meant to achieve. A final pirouette brought him to face them, his eyes alight.

"Will you dance it for me? Will you?"

With one voice, two world-famous dancers, fired with his vision, said—"When?"

"Ah, that! You know me! Maybe in a few months, maybe a year or two—you know how I work. But I'll call on you when the moment comes. Will you dance it for me then?"

They did indeed know how he worked, with what delight in the planning of each significant detail, with what absolute knowledge of what he wanted, and how he meant to achieve it. His enthusiasm and his ballet were both irresistible. Markova and Dolin agreed to dance for him and both regretted the engagements that later made the project impossible.

It would be a mistake to assume, as some do, that *Limelight* is Chaplin's swansong. There is no evidence of waning power in his work, or in his approach to it. There was a gap of seven years between *Modern Times* and *Monsieur Verdoux*: *Limelight* comes five years afterwards. His attack, his energy, ebullience, and dynamism are unimpaired. His attitude towards his work destroys any assumption that his career is ended, or that his present theme is significant of his awareness of its end. For, as he has so often said—"I don't get satisfaction out of my work—I get relief!"

Now that the stormy years are over, his life has settled down to a leisurely routine, broken by the sudden and imperious demands of his children. His day begins late, and is given over to periods of study or reading, followed by bouts of physical exercise; for Chaplin's early training in gymnastics and dancing, together with his vitality, have left him with a desire for hard exercise, on the tennis court or in the swimming pool.

For years now, his "brooding" period over his scenarios has been increasingly long and arduous, and he is never seen in his studios while he is enduring the initial torments of producing a theme. He has a full-time staff to deal with routine matters, and his technicians are always on call.

Music still fills a great part of Chaplin's life, in his own entertainment, the entertainment of his guests, and in his work. His attitude to his own music is best illustrated by his gesture to Markova. They had enjoyed together a lively discussion on *Monsieur Verdoux*. Markova had particularly liked the music Chaplin composed for the film, and Chaplin was delighted with her appreciation of it, in the same unbelieving way he had been delighted so many years before with the reception of the *Kid*. When she was about to leave Hollywood, he gave her a complete set of records of the music, because she had enjoyed it, and he had enjoyed making it.

The strain and suffering caused by the virulent hostility maintained against him by sections of the American public, has been largely, if not completely, overcome by the contentment of his private life. He is to-day leading the cultured and leisurely life of a wealthy man. His home, his wife, his family, his books, his music fill his days. He takes as long as he chooses over the preparation for, and working upon, each of his films. In his work, and in his home, he is at ease, after so many tormented years.

Perhaps the most revealing thing Chaplin has ever said, and the most typical, was the reply he gave to Sam Goldwyn's question—"What do you want most from the future?" Chaplin was a young man then, and he replied—"More life! Whether it comes through pictures or not—more life!" Anyone with such zest for living must either go under, or come out on top. And Chaplin, after titanic struggles, both personal and public, has come out on top.

For the past twelve years Chaplin has lived at peace in his beautiful Manoir de Ban at Vevey in Switzerland. The eight children of his marriage to Oona O'Neill have been brought up there, and the older ones are now launching out in their own careers. The eighteen-year-old girl who expressed her desire for a large family, and described her marriage to Chaplin as esoteric, has won this accolade from her husband after twenty years together: "I have the good fortune to be married to a wonderful wife. I wish I could write more about this, but it involves love, and perfect love is the most beautiful of all frustrations because it is more than one can express. As I live with Oona, the depth and beauty of her character are a continual revelation to me. Even as she walks ahead of me along the narrow sidewalks of Vevey with simple dignity, her neat little figure straight, her dark hair smoothed back, showing a few silver threads, a sudden wave of love and admiration comes over me for all that she is—and a lump comes into my throat."

PART TWO   ❦   CHAPLIN'S WORK

⟡ Experiment

ONE OF THE MAJOR INTERESTS OF CHAPLIN'S WORK IN FILM LIES in its subjective nature. It is the direct and astonishing expression of himself, and that factor gives homogeneity to all his films. From the guttersnipe malice of the Charlie of the Keystone Films has evolved the suave and subtle malice of Monsieur Verdoux. Between lies the evolution of a genius in terms of film.

In the year he spent under Mack Sennett at the Keystone Studios (1914-15), Chaplin learned the rudiments of film making, and how to transpose his own music-hall acts into film terms.

Standing out in bold relief against the background of ordinary slapstick, the figure of Charlie the little tramp, with his dancer's control of movement, and his astonishing agility, began to touch the hearts of his audiences with his laugh-provoking silhouette—the small bowler perched on a curly mop of hair, the tight short jacket buttoned over several waistcoats, the baggy trousers falling over the huge out-turned boots, the jaunty cane expressing every mood of its owner.

Gradually, Charlie was evolved. He emerges, at this stage, as an embodiment, in simple terms, of Chaplin's childhood. He is the White-chapel gutter urchin, always alert and on the offensive, malicious, faintly vicious, and with guttersnipe gestures—as when, in *Caught In A Cabaret* (1914), in a fight with Chester Conklin, he metamorphoses the slum nose prod, several times repeated, into a marvel of comic movement; or in *The Fatal Mallet* (1914) approaches an opponent with his backside jutting out from the waist in the manner of the slum gamecock.

Even in so early a stage, the little tramp is out of step with society, as the young Chaplin was out of step with his world. And from the beginning, Charlie is fastidious, a quality shown in the ragged elegance of his clothes, and in scenes where the little tramp brushes his clothes and polishes his nails with a scrubbing-brush; or delicately dips his finger tips in water after a meal of broken bits and pieces.

The Keystone films, now museum pieces, give us the childhood of Charlie the tramp—a figure of potentiality and promise rather than of achievement, feeling his way into the fantastic world prepared for him by the framework of Keystone comedy, out of step with that world, frustrated but never quite conquered by it.

The original elements in his work, that are dimly perceptible in the 35 Keystone Comedies—satire, lyricism, the malevolent life of inanimate objects, the humour of incongruity (as when he wears the bowler and spats with a leopard-skin in *His Prehistoric Past* (1914), —go side by side with the originality of his cinematic approach. At a time when the pioneers of film were applying stage technique to their work, Chaplin began to develop both plot and his own comedy line through movement and mime, to a shape that was rhythmically controlled.

When he transferred to the Essanay Company (1915), Chaplin continued to work along the lines he had discovered during his Keystone year. With his sixth film for that company—*The Tramp* (1915)—comes a change of major importance. For the first time, there is an undercurrent of pathos in the film. Until now, Charlie had evolved along the lines of urchinhood—vindictive, malicious, rebellious, his hand against everyone, and everyone's hand against his, ready to seize any advantage that would enable him to keep his precarious foothold on the fringes of society. In *The Tramp*, we see for the first time the pathetic outcast, the wanderer without friend or shelter, the displaced person of all time.

In this film, Charlie moved definitely from the category of comic type to that of personality, the eternal little fellow filled with a desire to love and be loved, for whom there is nothing but watching the fulfilment of others. Later in the Essanay year, with *The Bank* (1915) there comes a reiteration of the pathetic element in the little tramp, and a deepening of his personality.

After his first two years in film, Chaplin reaped the full harvest of the years that had preceded them, and then with the twelve films he made for the Mutual Company (1916-17), reached a peak in his creative life. These films were, in a special sense, the prototype of all that was to come from him; and his comedy is increasingly charged with a philosophical significance that lifts it out of farce into satire, and increases its pathos.

In the film world, other comedians—Buster Keaton with his deadpan face and robot-like gesture; Harold Lloyd with his owl-eyed glasses, and passion for suspending himself over space at dizzy heights; Ben Turpin of the crossed eyes, lamp-fringe moustache and romantic soul—made their audiences rock with laughter. Chaplin's greatness lies in the fact that he made his audiences laugh differently, made them "laugh lest they cry".

It was at this time that he embarked upon a patient research into comic effects, the essence of comedy, the reaction of audiences, with a view to discovering a more personal expression of humour. The Mutual films show the development of a subtler comedy, in which the controlled and rhythmic use of gesture is of prime importance.

There is development too in his use of décor. Until now, the background of his films had been largely háphazard, as it was for all American films in those early days. But with the Mutual series,

Chaplin used the décor of the film to provide an essential part of its atmosphere. The slum setting of *Easy Street* (1917), for example, not only adds incalculably to the effect of the theme of the film, but points its satire and its purpose in a way new, not only to Chaplin's work, but to American film-making generally.

The comedy types selected in the Essanay series—the Tough, the Policeman, the Young Girl, Charlie the Tramp—take on a deeper significance. They remain types in so far as they present the basic pattern of the film—Charlie the focal point of disturbance, continually harassed by power (The Tough) and authority (The Policeman), and continually transported into a world of delight and frustration because of his unrequited love for the Young Girl. But in the Mutual Series, both Charlie and the Girl acquire more complex personalities; and the Tough and the Policeman become symbols of forces greater than themselves.

Charlie's early malice and vivacity have now become satire, and indomitable optimism. Increasingly, he is the wistful, heart-catching clown, the hungry child pressing his nose against the pastrycook's window, the tramp forever lonely and alone, at odds with society. The Young Girl is no longer just beauty in distress, but a gentle and compassionate girl, the centre of Charlie's adventures and aspirations, who is regretfully unable to return his chivalric devotion.

As Charlie and the Girl acquire personality, and Charlie's absurd misadventures begin to take on a universal significance, the Tough and the Policeman are forced into new positions. Increasingly, as the Mutual films develop, they become symbols and agents of the avenging Fate predestined to pursue one end—the annihilation of Charlie.

Another interesting factor is by this time emerging. Chaplin had already made over fifty short films. The fundamental theme, common to them all, is the projection of his own childhood. His symbols are obvious—Charlie himself, lonely, outcast, tormented and unconquerable; Edna Purviance, the Young Girl—at once his mother, and all the unrealized and unattainable desires of childhood and adolescence; the Tough and the Policeman—the relentless forces of power and law and authority that shadowed those early years. The satire of these early films is the almost unconscious judgment of the adult Chaplin upon the cruelties he suffered in his youth.

Chaplin was now well away. His projection of his darkest hours was given in comedy so pointed and so ludicrous that great gales of laughter convulsed the whole world because of it. Charlie's personal idiosyncracies, his hilarious misadventures, the gallant battles he waged against impossible odds aroused great mirth; his wistfulness, his loneliness, the endless frustration of his loves and hopes and ambitions aroused compassion; and the jauntiness with which he faced up to the shattering blows of fate, his smallness in a world of mighty toughs and burly policemen, aroused something like admiration.

The Mutual films show clearly that Charlie is the doppelganger of Chaplin himself, and that his films are not only subjective, but in addition offer the lyrical and romantic presentation of his life. The films he had made to date were not simply a series of comedies different in kind and quality from any that had been made before. They were unique in that they were all linked, and traced the first cycle of the little Tramp's saga, an epic that covered the life of Chaplin himself. This gives them an homogeneity different from any other series of films made by the same man.

In 1917, at the end of his third year in films, and with the closing of the Mutual contract, all the elements of Chaplin's future work had been discovered and laid down. Every film afterwards with very few exceptions, will be a development of those elements, a contribution to the saga of Charlie, and evidence of Chaplin's mastery of the medium he made peculiarly his own.

✍ Development

IN 1918, CHAPLIN ACCEPTED THE CONTRACT OFFERED HIM BY THE First National Film Company, on terms that gave him complete freedom in his work. The films he made for this company have unhappily been withdrawn.

Among them, the trilogy—*A Dog's Life, Shoulder Arms* and *Sunnyside*—offer the fullest representation yet of the complex facets of Charlie's character, and therefore the most complete projection of Chaplin's essential self. *A Dog's Life* is primarily autobiography. The décor of the film reaches new heights, even for Chaplin, with its slum outskirts of an anonymous town, a no-man's-land of streets ending nowhere, or in vaguely defined waste spaces; a place of broken fences, melancholy, hopeless, despairing, with the miasma of abject poverty hanging over it. Here again is the adult Chaplin commenting on his own unhappy childhood, and this time taking it to the universal plane of the misery of all mankind. Though the film is a comedy, filled with side-splitting moments, the tragic undertones make themselves heard.

Shoulder Arms was made in the middle of 1918, and released shortly before the Armistice. In releasing it then, Chaplin gave proof of his own form of moral courage, that impelled him later, in sadly similar circumstances, to make and issue *The Great Dictator* in 1940, a year after England's declaration of war on Germany.

The anger and bitterness aroused by Chaplin's non-participation in the 1914-18 war had not abated when he released *Shoulder Arms,* and by so doing at once crystallized and justified the public statement he had made of his position.

This film also had a notable set—just trenches; but trenches that ooze from every sandbag, every monstrous mass of clay, every wall sweating moisture, a heavy effluvium of boredom and monotony.

Sunnyside came as an odd completion to this important trilogy. The desolate slum of *A Dog's Life,* the monstrous trenches of *Shoulder Arms* give way to an enchanted countryside shimmering under the rays of a magical sun. In spite of its comedy and burlesque, in spite of its half-hearted attempt to satirise a type of pastoral film popular at the time, *Sunnyside* is unique among all Chaplin's films for its highly developed poetic quality.

These three films, ranging from stark realism to sunlit fantasy, from almost epic sorrow to the most light-hearted gaiety, are a multiple expression of Charlie's complete personality. In them are presented the solitary outcast generated in misery and poverty, despised and rejected of men; the valiant little Greatheart, Don Quixote; and the idealist poet. Linking these manifestations together is our realization that Charlie is more than Charlie, more than Chaplin. Since Chaplin first projected himself in the likeness of Charlie across the screens of the world, Charlie has grown, for all his littleness, to the stature of a Colossus. Genius outstrips its creation; and Charlie, arising directly out of Chaplin's personal saga, served to make that saga universal and eternal until we have, with this trilogy, the representative of all mankind.

The ground now was prepared for *The Kid,* perhaps the best known and best remembered of Chaplin's earlier films.

The theme of the film—the abandonment of an unwanted child, its reluctant adoption by Charlie, and their hazardous life together until the child, together with Charlie, is restored to his now famous and wealthy mother, is elementary and banal in its facile appeal to the emotions. But Chaplin, employing all his wealth of comedy, tragedy, and pathos, made of it a film of great beauty and tenderness.

As in all his films—and this is one of the factors that put him in a class of his own—the obvious development of the film and its story reveal another and parallel development. The Kid—played so superbly by Jackie Coogan—is clearly another presentation of Charlie, so that we have in this film a dual personality, the adult and the child Charlie, and in both the same heart-catching quality.

The Kid is an extension of *A Dog's Life,* and the dual presentation of the waif motif increases its desolation, as it increases its comedy.

At the end of the film, when Charlie has been cruelly awakened from his blissful dream by his old enemy the Policeman, to find that the Kid has been received into the sheltering arms of his mother, there is a moment of poignancy when Charlie realizes that those arms are willing to take him in also. His incredulity, bewilderment, dawning belief, and radiance, catch at the heartstrings, for Charlie has such unappeasable needs.

With *The Pilgrim* Chaplin finished the series of films he was due to make for the First National Company. This film proves definitely that Charlie now is adult. The simplicities of childhood where much is hidden that cannot be expressed; the hesitations and confusions of adolescence, have yielded place to the full emergence of a personality as subtle and complex as Chaplin's own.

Creator and creation, Chaplin and Charlie, are so closely linked as to be almost indivisible. In both, early promise has been vitally fulfilled, development of personality and artistry has reached great peaks. Chaplin is ripe now for his major films, and Charlie is no longer the youngest clown, but the greatest clown of all.

After *The Pilgrim*, which was released in 1922, Chaplin was at last free to consider his future work with the United Artists Company, which he had formed three years before with Mary Pickford, Douglas Fairbanks, and D. W. Griffiths.

His work for United Artists, from *A Woman Of Paris,* released in 1923, to *Monsieur Verdoux* (1947), his last film to date, shows the irresistible evolution of his genius in its highest form. All that Chaplin had ever done in cinema, from the first curio *Making A Living,* of 1914, through all the years of apprenticeship and experiment, was given in these great films what would seem to be its final and fullest form.

Chaplin had progressively increased the range of his work, and the time taken over it, so that in the period 1923-1947, he produced seven major films, which fall into two groups.

With one significant exception, Charlie the tramp is the hero of them all, a maturer Charlie, more human, more eloquent, less sublime. In the earlier group, he is tortured through his own humanity, exposed to greed, loneliness, malice, poverty; with man and nature both against him, finding shelter nowhere, nowhere any peace or any hope. The hopelessness of Charlie breaks through his former optimism until, in *City Lights* (1931), the last of this group, it cuts the future from beneath his feet, as the blind flower girl whose sight has been restored through Charlie's efforts, sees her benefactor, and laughs at the comic sight he makes.

The last three films, *Modern Times* (1936), *The Great Dictator*

(1940), *Monsieur Verdoux* (1947) show another Charlie yet—the ardent crusader, who was there from the beginning, expressing with sly pantomime, with sharp satire, with humour and ridicule, his profound awareness and hatred of cruelty, vice and misery, of vanity, oppression, and the orgiastic destruction of war. All his work is an expression of a fundamental love of humanity, and hatred of its oppressors; all his work is a preparation for his annihilation of soulless industrialization in *Modern Times*; for the thunderous eloquence of his overthrow of fascism in *The Great Dictator*; for the cold, clear judgment of modern society, with its callous indifference to human dignity, security and life itself, that is the essence of *Monsieur Verdoux*, the apotheosis of them all, Charlie in his ultimate form to date.

Achievement

IT IS CURIOUS THAT THE FIRST FILM CHAPLIN MADE FOR UNITED Artists was a mordant tragedy, from which Charlie was banished. Throughout the early work of Chaplin, the underlying tragic note has grown in insistence. From the beginning, Chaplin wished to make a tragedy, as fragments of a serious film to be called *Life*, dating from 1915, can testify; an ambition to produce, not to play, Hamlet. It is possible that he wished to show Hollywood, who now tended to despise comedy, that he was capable of making a great and serious film; and it was well known that he had for a long time wished to give Edna Purviance a leading rôle of major importance. She was, as an artist, almost entirely the work of his hands, and he wanted to try her in an exacting part. Chaplin called upon all his great artist's patience, summoned all his gift, all his technique, to create what he clearly intended to be his tragic masterpiece; and produced by the end of 1923, *A Woman Of Paris*, a work of unyielding pessimism, filled with a cruel and biting irony unlike any that had yet come from him.

Apart from its significance in Chaplin's evolution as an artist, the film had a very great influence on cinema. It was an original film from which a school of cinematic art was derived—the ancestor of sophisticated drama in film; the progenitor of all films dealing with psychological complexity. It was also the forerunner of simplicity of technique, the paring down to essentials that had always been typical of Chaplin's work, and which was destined to overthrow the fussy and complicated overstatement of early American film. This bareness of effect, so brilliantly successful in Chaplin's hands, counteracted the excessive use of technical effects much favoured at that time. Moreover, as Seldes points out "When Chaplin made *A Woman of Paris* as producer and director, it was considered an idiosyncrasy, almost as if he had chosen to do manual labour"; but the film gained because of it, and his example was followed by others.

By the spring of 1924, Chaplin had started work on *The Gold Rush,* and in due course released what was to become his best-loved film, not excepting even *The Kid.*

The visual beauty of *The Gold Rush* transcends even its comedy. Chaplin the poet saw the grandeur of the snow plains of Alaska as his décor, and put up against that dazzling expanse the black, dwarfed file of prospectors, the silhouette of Charlie, the burly outlines of Mack Swain. The film is a panorama in black and white, the most absolute use of the obvious resources of film that had ever been made, and the most successful. The décor thoughtfully provided by Nature and Chaplin's poetic imagination, plays a decisive part in the film. The white unbroken snows give an impression of solitude, of eternity, of man's littleness in the vast scheme of the universe. Against it, Charlie's small, gallant silhouette stands out in sharp relief— as when he sits forlorn in the middle of the empty plain, equipped for prospecting by the addition of a shawl to his bowler, cane and baggy trousers. The log cabin, where most of the drama is to be enacted, achieves greater prominence because of this opposition of black and white. Even the cosy warmth of the saloon is enhanced because of the cold, still snows looming under a heavy sky just outside.

Tragedy and comedy are so blended in *The Gold Rush* that the audience is kept throughout on the border-line between laughter and tears, the most perfect balance yet achieved by this tight-rope walker, expert in treading delicately on the verge of the opposite emotions.

Charlie is a complete person here, filled with a rich humanity that strips him entirely of his earlier fantasy, his poetry, his almost mytho-logical presentation. Now his feet are firmly rooted on earth, in the snow. And he, who has always been up against society, is now up against nature itself. The perils and dangers that have always beset him are transmuted now from falling into ponds and being chased by policemen, into avalanches that carry his log cabin to the very edge of a precipice, where he rocks half-suspended over infinite space; or great black bears that dog his unknowing footsteps.

Chaplin's building of the scenes, from the time of the snow-storm that shuts up the three prospectors in a small cabin amid the vast, oppressive silence of the snows, grows in tension to generate the gradual compelling hatred of each for the others. This building of tension continues between the two remaining after one has gone to seek help, based on a theme of hunger and fear. Comes the unforget-able scene of the stewed boots, consumed with grace, elegance, and difficulty by Charlie; the scenes that create an intense feeling of

Charlie. The sadness and solitude of the clown

The Pilgrim (1923) The Gold Rush (1925)

Three aspects of Charlie

The Circus (1928)

Verdoux. Charlie with his desires realized

Lust for Power. The Great Dictator (1940)

The "Charlie" Clown. Charlie Rivels

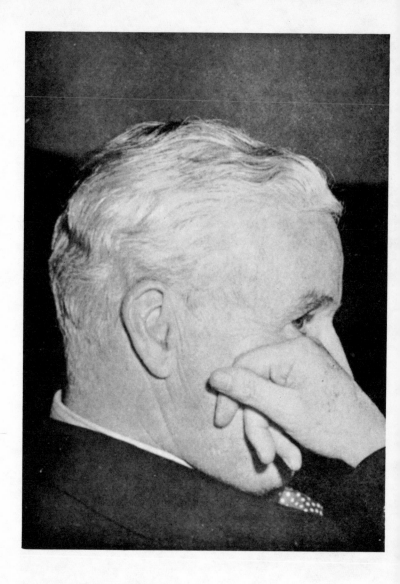

The Man behind the Mask

nervous panic, when things take on a malignant energy that forces him into terror—the bar that drops suddenly upon his head, the stove that burns him when he tries to avoid the bar; and then, when the feeling of panic is at its height, his companion goes mad, thinks Charlie is a chicken and tries to kill and eat him. It is a parody of the strong, silent man type of drama; it is also a bitter commentary on the hostility of men towards each other.

Having created his peak of tension, Chaplin lets the film down gently into sentimentality and pathos. Charlie is drawn to his fellow men as the moth to the candle flame; and we are given the incomparable shot of him just outside the threshold of the saloon, leaning slightly on his cane, the other hand hanging limp. All his bitter solitude is in that pose, and all his unsatisfied longing in the look he bends on Georgia Hale when he first catches sight of her. All his frustration is in the fact that she smiles at others, but does not see him. Charlie has travelled a long way from the guttersnipe of the Keystone days.

Moment of Defeat

AS SOON AS "THE GOLD RUSH" WAS FINISHED, CHAPLIN SOUGHT FOR the inspiration of his next film. A factor of interest in tracing the evolution of his genius lies in the recurrence of certain themes that have been in his mind for years, some eventually being used, others partly used, others never actually touched upon. We have seen how his desire to make a serious film brought about the fragmentary *Life* in 1915 and *A Woman Of Paris* in 1923. An unpublished short, *The Suicide*, of early date, provided a basis for the scenes of the intended suicide in *City Lights* (1931). Amongst the most significant of the recurring motifs are those of Napoleon and Jesus Christ. The former dates back in spirit to the days of his childhood, when he played the Napoleon and led his fellow urchins into battle against their kind. Later, the desire to make a film on Napoleon gained increasing strength. Chaplin wished to present him not as a powerful general, but as "a sickly being, taciturn, almost morose, continually harassed by the members of his family". Here surely is an interesting transposition of self; and it may well be that the uprising and spread of fascism in Europe cured him of his passion for Napoleon; for certainly the nearest approach to the desired film of his hero is to be found in *The Great Dictator,* under the sign of the Double Cross!

It is a tragedy that the increased hostility, latent and overt, surrounding him and all that he does and is, will probably prevent him from ever accomplishing a film based on the life of Jesus Christ, about whom he writes in these terms—"I believe that the most powerful, most dynamic, the most important person who has ever lived has been terribly deformed by tradition. . . . No one would prevent me from considering him as a splendid man, virile, full blooded, to whom one turns instinctively when one is in trouble. . . . If I could produce a film on the story of Christ, I would show him welcomed with delirious joy by men, women and children; they would throng round him in order to feel his magnetism. Not at all a sad, pious, and stiff person, but a lonely man who has been the most misunderstood of all time".

In search now of a theme, he chose one he had formerly called *The Clown* and now renamed *The Circus,* in which Charlie found himself lonely amid the exuberant gaiety of circus folk. Charlie's clowning was never so filled with grief as in *The Circus.* The framework of the film, its circus background, caused Chaplin to revert to a farcical comedy derived from his earlier days; but this serves only to point the deep sadness of the little clown, which pervades the whole film.

Here Charlie is presented as a Don Quixote without exuberance or fire, Lewis Carroll's White Knight, adrift in the incomprehensible callousness of life. Only his essential resignation enables him to go on living in the alien world. Insensibly, as the film progresses, he becomes the symbol of goodness struggling against all the evil and stupidity of the world. Charlie has shed for all time his precociousness, his malice, his knavery.

The making of this film coincided with Chaplin's divorce from Lita Grey, and was indeed interrupted by the repercussions of the case and its effect on Chaplin. Certainly, in the presentation of Charlie in *The Circus,* Chaplin seems to be compensating himself. The film is heavy with the strain and fatigue he was undergoing at the time of its making, as for so long before. Charlie has lost his zest, his optimism, and has acquired instead an intense and resigned sadness. The lyrical quality of his work is concealed beneath a bitter philosophy, the poet overlaid by the satirist.

His next film, *City Lights* (1931), released at a moment when wild enthusiasm for the new talking pictures was sweeping across the continents, presents once more the complete personality of Charlie, and what has clearly become the reiterated and significant symbols of Chaplin's work—the idealist tramp with his unquenchable love, compassion, chivalry and goodness; the Girl, in this case blind, who is complementary to him, in need of his devotion and herself submissive, feminine and unattainable. The eccentric millionaire upon whom their fates depend is a new form of the *deus ex machina,* changing the social forces that beset and overwhelm them according to his incalculable whim.

City Lights shows an increase in the sadness of Charlie. Instead of his former jauntiness, his indifference to fate, his uncontrollable irony, there is a lassitude, an acceptance of unhappiness that was first indicated in *The Gold Rush* (1925), then came to shadow *The Circus* (1928), and finally in *City Lights* (1931) took so prominent a place it was as though Chaplin were expressing through Charlie the impact of cataclysmic effects in his own life and in the world of film—his unsavoury divorce case, and the coming of talkies.

To the Charlie of *City Lights* Alexander Woolcott's eulogy most properly belongs—"It must be said of Chaplin that he has created only one character, but that one, in his matchless courtesy, in his unfailing gallantry—his preposterous, innocent gallantry, in a world of gross Goliaths—that character is, I think, the finest gentleman of our time".

Mastery

ALL CHAPLIN'S WORK IS MARKED WITH TREMENDOUS FEELING, sometimes translated into terms of sentimentality and pathos, always vital and effective. As he gained in technique, experience, and financial and artistic independence, so he was able to express more fully the torrent of feeling within him. The torment and tempest of his own life, the active and increasing hostility against him in America, affected, but did not check the torrent. These factors served to increase the tragic feeling in his work, made him reaffirm his identity with the underdog, caused him to clarify his feelings about society, about mankind, about the universe.

In his last three films, he has made his unequivocal statements of his most passionate concern for humanity, and equally passionate hatred of all that impedes mankind in its struggle to survive. That this hatred was still expressed with hilarious comedy is part of the miracle of genius.

Five years elapsed between the release of *City Lights* (1931) and that of *Modern Times* (1936); and the latter is evidence that in that intervening period, Chaplin recovered fully from the events that threatened to overcome him in the earlier years of his work with United Artists. The Charlie of *City Lights* was as nearly defeated as we had ever seen him, left cruelly without illusion or dream to sustain him at the end, as Chaplin himself had been left.

Modern Times is as glowing with vitality and optimism, impertinence and humour, as *City Lights* was shadowed with lassitude, pessimism and pain. There could not be greater contrast in mood than there is between these two films chronologically next to each other. It is as if Chaplin had overcome all his uncertainty concerning the introduction of dialogue into film, all his suffering over the calamitous ending of his second marriage, and had expressed this newly-acquired release in the dynamism and gaiety of this film.

The Chaplin hallmark is put upon the film from the opening shot of sheep rushing through a gate, followed by one of workers coming up out of a subway; and by the stupendous satire of the factory décor, shining, sterile, inhuman, endlessly working at producing nothing. Charlie the intractable, Charlie the independent spirit, has become a factory hand. But Charlie never can be a factory worker. He demonstrates his incapacity, and incidentally satirizes the inhuman mechanisation of industry, by failing to tighten a bolt on the endless conveyor belt. This small failure in routine upsets the whole complicated process until Charlie is caught in the machinery—only to demonstrate that if cogwheels are large enough, one may safely stroll among them, a ludicrous and brilliant anticlimax. In *Modern Times,* Charlie comes across another waif, a rebellious little guttersnipe, as different from gentle submissive Edna as any personality could be, the part admirably played by Paulette Goddard. In *The Kid,* Chaplin offered a dual presentation of the tramp, in childhood and maturity. Now he offers a parallel presentation of two waifs, outcast from society, and frustrated in every attempt to secure their modest needs—a roof, food, and privacy. Every effort to secure their dream ends in the Black Maria; until at the end they go off jauntily towards the horizon, towards the unknown; and this time Charlie takes his female counterpart with him.

There were many who wished to see a fundamentally political significance in this harsh criticism of modern times, this ironic indictment of the slavery of the machine. Quite apart from the fact that it is an absurdity to reduce to terms of political propaganda a work of art which shows at one level Charlie's perpetual resistance to mass law; and at another the incapacity of society to supply the urgent needs of its people, we have Chaplin's own, constantly reiterated plea, formulated once more in 1947—"For pity's sake, let's stop mixing up art with the shady political intrigues which go on all over the world".

The evidence of the film itself does not support any opinion, adverse or laudatory, implying political bias. The worker, the sheeplike worker of the opening shots, the striker who follows any leader who happens to have a flag, is satirized as incisively as any other aspect of existence that earns Chaplin's condemnation.

In this film Chaplin, as always, is expressing his feeling and his credo in human and universal, not in political, terms. His Little Man, with his female counterpart, is seeking man's minimum requirements and is frustrated in the search through the soulless and inhuman demands of bigger and better production; the submerging of the individual in the mass.

The Great Dictator (1940) released four years after *Modern Times,* was an inevitable sequel to the film in which he attacked and satirized a form of civilization which deprived mankind of its basic needs.

In 1918, in the weary last year of the first world-war, *Shoulder Arms* set the very trenches rocking with laughter. Now, in the first year of the war against Fascism, Chaplin stripped the megalomaniacs of Germany and Italy of their delusion of grandeur and shrivelled them to Carlyle's "forked radishes" through the mockery of laughter.

Hugh Kingsmill, in an interesting portrait of Charlie Chaplin, symbol of the weary disillusioned Little Man of Western Europe, suffering from the social disintegration following the 1914-1918 war, draws the following parallel between Chaplin and Hitler—"What the Little Man of the 'Gold Rush' desired was money and women, what Hitler desired was power, these desires forming together the sum of what most men want from the world. Hitler, who was born in the same week of April, 1889, as Chaplin, was his complement, not his antithesis, the Napoleon of mass consciousness as Chaplin was its Byron."

There is something that excites the imagination in the thought of these two world famous men, born in the same month of the same year in similar poverty and obscurity, pursuing their parallel destinies from opposite aims, the one driven by hatred, the other by compassion, until, in their maturity and universal fame, Hitler exerted all his power to conquer the world; while Chaplin, having already conquered the world, destroyed, with the power of laughter, the pretensions of the other Little Man.

Chaplin had always been interested in the dictator mentality: and Sam Goldwyn said of him, "Chaplin loves power—as no one else whom I have ever seen loves it". There was in him a natural understanding upon which to base his acute and brilliant study of Adenoid Hynkel, the man in whom love of power derived from knowledge of lack of power and had become megalomania. "Hitler, to me, beneath that stern and foreboding appearance he gives in news reels and news photos, actually is a small, mean and petty neurasthenic. Mussolini suggests an entirely different character—loud, noisy, boastful, a peasant at heart." Here, in Chaplin's own words, is the genesis of Hynkel and Napaloni.

The comedy of the film is all contained in the part dealing with the dictators; its sentimentality and pathos are expressed in terms of the little Jewish barber, an oddly foreshortened view of Charlie, and Hannah, the Jewish girl he befriends. The opposition of the dictator and the barber, which is the core of the film and its indictment of tyrants, is underlined by Chaplin's masterly use of speech. From the dictator pours a torrent, a spate, a flood of words, picked up and magnified by microphones and loudspeakers, denunciatory and hysterical, a prominent element in the caricature. The little barber scarcely speaks at all, and still expresses himself mainly through gesture, as Charlie always did. The two personalities are brilliantly presented in terms of speech; and this is the more remarkable when we realize that this is Chaplin's *first* talking film.

One other interesting point arising from the use Chaplin makes of speech in his first talkie, lies in the effect it has upon Charlie. Already, in appearing as the Jewish barber, antithesis of Hynkel, member of a persecuted people, Charlie has lost some of his transcendental quality, his universality. He loses more now that speech has come to him. Charlie expressed the whole of himself and of mankind in mime. Words impede and embarass him; and we feel, with a nostalgia keen as pain, that the Charlie we knew has gone from us.

A major part of the film is given to Charlie's recurrent yearning for the little home, the plot of land, roots in the earth, harbourage and rest, which first made its tentative appearance as early in the saga as 1915, in *The Tramp*; and which has reappeared, in one form or another, at intervals ever since, from *A Dog's Life* to *City Lights*, until in *Modern Times* it was nakedly presented as the simple aspiration of all men. Now, in *The Great Dictator,* this yearning is crystallized, illuminated and explained as part of the Jewish tragedy, the despairing cry of the persecuted race. The second part of the film is wholly dominated by this dream of the Promised Land, which, as so much else in Chaplin's work, is at once intensely personal to him; and a presentation of the age-old problem that has contemporary significance.

The end of the film was so unexpected that most reviewers, and some critics, were taken aback, and Chaplin was severely trounced for betraying the artistic unity and integrity of his work. The little Jewish barber, forced to impersonate Hynkel, is called upon to deliver one of the famous harangues. Without warning or preparation, Chaplin himself suddenly takes over. Satire, ridicule, comedy, pathos, the dualism and opposition of the main characters all forgotten, Chaplin the crusader speaks to mankind with burning sincerity, with absolute simplicity, with resolute rhetoric, taking as his large theme the brotherhood of man.* The screen is filled with the gigantic mask, not of

* See Appendix B.

Charlie nor of Hynkel, but of Chaplin; the voice is the ardent voice of Chaplin, and the torrent of feeling is his own, with a tremendous impact and power. We are reminded of Roger Manvell's comment that Chaplin's philosophy is so deeply felt that it is becoming "almost messianic".

Modern Times and *The Great Dictator* both bore witness to the fact that Chaplin had formulated the ideas hovering on the verge of full expression in all his films from the beginning. His dispersed and tentative, almost oblique, attack on the society of his time was defined in both; and they each contained the most complete presentation of the dualism in Charlie, first seen in *The Kid*. In *Modern Times,* Charlie discovered his feminine counterpart; in *The Great Dictator,* the duality was expressed more subtly still in opposite terms—the little Jewish barber, and Hynkel who sought to destroy him, representing an opposition in Chaplin's own character, the opposite sides of his own qualities and defects.

Earlier in his career, Chaplin had made a series of films that formed a trilogy that was in effect the summing-up of his work in film to that date—*A Dog's Life* (1918), *Shoulder Arms* (1918), *Sunnyside* (1919). Eighteen years later, the pattern repeats itself. With *Modern Times* (1936) he begins another trilogy destined to include *The Great Dictator* (1940) and *Monsieur Verdoux* (1947), and to provide a second and maturer summing-up.

Monsieur Verdoux

IN SPITE OF THE YEARS BETWEEN "MODERN TIMES" (1936) AND *Monsieur Verdoux* (1947) the films in this second trilogy tread upon each other's heels; and in *Monsieur Verdoux,* Chaplin brings to a head his attack on society, and the significance of the repeated dualism in Charlie.

It is easier to understand *Monsieur Verdoux,* and to begin to appreciate the countless ramifications of its theme, and the artistry of its presentation, when it is analysed in its relation to Chaplin's total work, which is itself the exact expression of his own reaction to the experiences and feeling of his life. Many of Chaplin's admirers were disappointed in *Monsieur Verdoux,* many others bewildered. This was largely due to a failure to understand that here was not an isolated film, with Chaplin playing a new part in a somewhat macabre plot. It was the latest stage of Chaplin's continued attack upon society, begun in his first films, gaining in anger and ardour and impetus through the years, increased by his own persecution until, in these last three films he decisively gave tongue to his hatred.

Monsieur Verdoux can be no disappointment to those who have followed the unhesitating course of Chaplin's artistic and personal evolution; it becomes for them a fulfilment of promise, rich in symbolism. It is a major paradox, more subtle than anything Chaplin ever did before.

Much was made of the fact that Chaplin was said to have based the film upon Landru, but it would be as absurd to overestimate the importance of sources in this case as in Shakespeare's. The outline of the character Verdoux is similar to that of Landru, a similar social psychology serves to explain them both; and they were both excellent family men! Landru's "magnetic eye" is gloriously caricatured in Verdoux's seduction scenes. But that is all, and it was clearly never Chaplin's purpose to present a bowdlerized life of Landru.

A source of greater significance in the film is to be found in an element drawn from modern American society—the preponderance of wealthy widows who form a parasitic shell upon the living organism of Society, maintaining their wealth at all costs while contributing nothing to the organism supporting them. Verdoux's murders are a symbol of Chaplin's desire to exterminate the parasites, who, by their very existence, force wide open the gap between wealth and poverty, take away Verdoux's cherished home and reduce thousands like him to penury. This desire is stimulated no doubt by his romanticism towards women, prone to turn to bitter hatred of those among them who tried to destroy him.

Once the social scene is set, Chaplin drives home his condemnation of its folly and evil by taking its guiding principles to their logical limit. That indifference to individual liberty, callousness towards human suffering, carelessness towards life itself, that are for him the basic factors in modern society become part and parcel of Verdoux's *modus vivendi*. Forced into an impasse by social chaos, he applies the principles underlying that chaos to secure for himself and his family an adequate livelihood. So that finally, society, in condemning him, condemns itself; in destroying him, implies the necessity for its own destruction; in denouncing him as anti-social, reduces itself to terms of anarchy. Therein lies the essential paradox of *Monsieur Verdoux*; and the core of Chaplin's most scathing indictment of the times in which we live.

Another interesting aspect of the film lies in its presentation of Charlie and his duality, the subtlest yet. For Verdoux is the little tramp in reverse, the other side of Charlie.

Chaplin has in his possession thousands of feet of film of himself in magnificent costumes, the perfect dandy. That fact is significant, taken with the ragged elegance of the little tramp of the early films, and the aristocratic dignity contrasting so absurdly with his outcast state. In *City Lights*, Charlie wore tails with an air, knew how to drive a Rolls, and smoke an expensive cigar; and many years before that, Chaplin had told H. G. Wells, "I have always desired to look natty"; and described with detail and affection his attempts to look a "masher" for the young Hetty of his early love affair.

There lies the clue to Verdoux, who is Charlie with his desires realized. Verdoux has the elegance Charlie longed for; the beautiful little home, gentle wife, and healthy son that Charlie dreamed of. Verdoux has an established position in the society Charlie only saw from the outside. Charlie desired women, Verdoux conquers them. Charlie was terrified of policemen, and ran away from them; Verdoux makes fools of them, and then gives himself into their hands. Charlie walked off cheerfully into the unknown, and so did Verdoux, but with a difference. Verdoux is then the other face of Charlie, but with the same doom upon him. Destiny, once more in the guise of social forces, threatens to snatch from him these realized desires—home, wealth, position, elegance. And Verdoux the cynic, reinforced by Charlie the sentimentalist, fights Society with its own weapons in a desperate attempt to retain his dreams at last made real.

The dualism of Charlie is at its most subtle in this film, for it lies within Verdoux himself, where good and evil are united. In its earliest form this dualism was simply another demonstration of the waif motif, with evil an exterior force. But Charlie, growing older and wiser, realized the evil that lies within. Charlie and the Kid, Charlie and the girl waif, were against Society. Then Charlie became at once the symbol of a persecuted race, and of the tyranny that oppressed it, as though Chaplin were aware that even Charlie could not escape his share of responsibility for social chaos. Now, in *Monsieur Verdoux* he has united the antagonists in one person.

Verdoux the home lover, the family man, accepts society's vicious terms, to become Verdoux the male prostitute and murderer; Chaplin has made the enormous step forward, the realization of the latent evil in each one of us, ready to flower in its proper soil. Charlie the pure in heart can become Verdoux the amoralist, given wrong conditions.

The antagonists then dwell together; so that when Verdoux meets the young girl waif, down and out, yet still filled with faith in humanity, he cannot kill her, because there is in her the essence of the little tramp. One part of Verdoux recognizes her; and renders the other powerless against her.

Through his very existence, Verdoux makes Society aware of its guilt (much as Chaplin is an ever present thorn in the flesh of

American Society). He is therefore condemned to death, with all the trappings of justice, through much the same impulse that brings about a declaration of war, when no reasonable solution can be found for political or economic chaos.

Should anyone doubt that Verdoux is Charlie, fighting with new and more sinister weapons his lifelong battle, the last scene of the film must dispel his uncertainty. For as we watch him go out to the guillotine, a small, ageing man with drooping shoulders, back to the camera, between two gendarmes, we are irresistibly compelled to remember the little tramp setting off jauntily to the unknown horizon, to new adventure. There is the sudden catching at the heart again, and this time with the revelation—that the road leading nowhere, along which the little tramp so often set out with a jaunty whirling of his cane at the end of his films—led in the end to death. The Policeman has caught up with Charlie; and Fate, in the shape of Society, has annihilated him at last. We do not quite know whether Charlie or Society has won the last round of a contest that has been fiercely and comically waged for nearly forty years.

The Elegant Melancholy of Twilight

THE SAGA OF CHARLIE, THAT GREAT EPIC POEM WITH WHICH CHAPLIN was preoccupied throughout his career, seemed to have ended with the execution of Verdoux. But Charlie, whose whole life had been an endless struggle against vicissitudes that would have defeated a lesser man, was not to be destroyed without a final struggle; and in Chaplin's next film there was a strange and ghostly resurgence of Charlie.

Superficially, *Limelight*, released in 1952, was the story of a clown, Calvero, an aging, out-of-work music hall comedian, once the top of the bill, who saved a young dancer from suicide, restored her faith and her career, and himself died during a benefit performance given on his behalf. The film provoked laughter and tears, divided the critics, and confounded those among them who had believed *Monsieur Verdoux* to be Chaplin's swan song.

On this same level, it seems to be a film apart, different in kind and content from all the others, one of the most moving and somehow the most curious. For a closer inspection showed that it was in fact a nostalgic summing up of all the rest, and the one in which the ghost of Charlie left the body of Chaplin in a final dramatic dissolution of a long duality.

Whatever Chaplin's intention—and his intentions are, in his films, meticulously carried out and then transformed by his peculiar genius into something rich and strange—Calvero is Chaplin himself. For the first time we see him on the screen as he really is—a small man, moving beautifully, neat and quick, with silver hair and exquisite hands: with a dignified manner masking an ineradicable diffidence, with a quiet warm voice and a dynamic presence, muted for the part, but bursting out irrepressibly in moments of sudden gaiety or mimicry that enliven a sober discussion. And when Calvero speaks of "the elegant melancholy of twilight" in an attempt to brush off his own private spooks, it is Chaplin speaking his awareness of a special atmosphere in time, and one that lifts the film into a poetic fusion of past and present.

The nostalgia of the film streams from this Chaplin-Calvero. This is not in fact the London of 1914 or thereabouts, but Chaplin's memory of its shoddy music halls and downgraded comic turns, the shabby boarding houses filled with old pro's keeping up appearances or giving up the ghost, the nameless streets of squalid houses, littered with sad refuse, smoke-filled pubs, grimy children clustering round the hurdy-gurdy man, the chill and fear of poverty remembered from a distance and given a sad, haunting beauty by the man who knew it all too well.

Calvero talks endlessly to his young ballerina when she is convalescent. Some of the talk is confused, or banal; some clear and direct; or simple and moving—"Truth is all I want, and if possible a little dignity." And the bittersweet philosophy, at once personal and limited, general and wide open, that is expressed is the one that Chaplin has evolved for himself from the experiences of his turbulent life, now that he is a little withdrawn from them "in the elegant melancholy of twilight." All this is Chaplin, with no vestige of Charlie left in him.

But Charlie is there too, a haunting presence whenever Calvero, in his dreams or in reality, performs one of his music hall turns. It is as though Charlie, if he must accept the fact of his death, is determined to have one last fling. He is there in the absurdity of a dapper, full ringmaster costume, complete with brutal upturned moustache and long whip—for a flea circus. He appears dressed as a Grimaldi clown in the ballet sequence; a tattered vagabond in a jaunty straw hat; a pub busker in a coat of many colours, like Harlequin in a top hat. And in the various performances, the whole of Charlie is there, from the earliest slapstick days through the pathos and defiance of the little tramp to the anger and bitterness of Verdoux, haunting the song and dance and mimicry of Calvero on stage and looking sometimes with sick eyes on the cruelty of man towards his fellow man.

This is the only time Chaplin and Charlie have been separate, and this separation is made absolute at the end of the film.

Calvero is given a benefit performance, arranged by his friends, and his own act, an hilariously funny music hall turn partnered by Buster Keaton, ends with him falling into a drum. Calvero triumphantly reaches the conclusion of his act, falls expertly into the drum, and there suffers a heart attack. And there the agonised eyes of Charlie look out of Calvero's clown mask; by the time Calvero is carried into the wings to watch the little dancer make her entrance, Charlie has gone forever, and Chaplin has taken over. The make-up is removed from the dying face, the spotlight following his young dancer as she glides across the stage shines upon the nimbus of his silver hair: and he shows in death the dignity he yearned for.

Limelight exorcised the ghost of Charlie in an evocative film of beauty and sadness. A *King in New York*, Chaplin's first film made in England and released in 1957, will perhaps prove to have been a transitional work, the first from which the little tramp was wholly absent.

✎ Charlie

CHARLIE IS THE UNIQUE EXPRESSION OF THE POETIC AND THE PHILO-sophic art of Chaplin, the focal point of so many planes of experience, thought, and emotion, at once personal to Chaplin and common to humanity, that he is more gargantuan than any creature of Rabelais.

The poetic quality of Charlie developed early in his saga. It is most evident in his movement, that was never clumsy or uncontrolled in the early slapstick days, and that became increasingly a delight to watch as his character developed. It reached its fullest expression in the balletic shaping of films like *The Champion* (1915) and *One A.M.* (1916), and in the dance sequences contained in several of his early films, notably *Sunnyside* (1919). Charlie dancing is Charlie liberated from all corporeal burdens, a lyrical expression of the spirit of the little tramp that transcends his outward manifestation; for remember that Charlie dances in the grotesque vestments of the tramp.

On a similar plane, the several dream sequences in Charlie's films —in *The Bank* (1915), *Sunnyside* (1919), *The Kid* (1921) have all the same lyrical quality. Charlie enters into a fantastic world remote from the sorrows of mankind, the travail of society, and the burden of his own solitude. Those are specific elements in the poetic pilgrimage of the little tramp, who throughout the whole course of his film life, pursues the unattainable, so expressing the deepest hunger of the human spirit. His attitude to life—the appraisal and rejection of Society, his constant quest for something greater than himself, some object of devotion—is as poetic as Galahad's search for the Holy Grail. Indeed, Charlie is "a very parfit, gentil Knight" as the shrewd but kindly eye of Dan Chaucer would have known him.

His dancing, his dreams, his pursuit of the unattainable, are all poetic; and so is Charlie himself. He is outside Society as a child is outside, a law unto himself, unaware of any moral or ethical significance but his own, applying to his environment a child's absolute judgment. Through those clear eyes, sometimes puzzled, sometimes wistful, sometimes ironic, we see ourselves in all our human frailty, but with its emphasis shifted, so that it is all a little ridiculous, as well as moving. We look upon ourselves with Charlie's vision, with irony and compassion, as though we were entirely detached from our own activities.

Chaplin's art is philosophic as well as poetic; Charlie is more therefore than an endearing little fellow, or a lyrical dancer, or a clown. When, in *The Tramp* (1915) Charlie set off down that long road, dejectedly at first, then with jaunty eagerness to seek unknown adventure; when, in *The Bank* (1915) he suddenly looked·out upon the audience with eyes holding the age-long grief of man, he began to take on the universal quality that was to lift him among the immortals. While Charlie blundered and failed, evaded cops, cuckolded husbands in imagination if not in fact, fell into ponds, tumbled downstairs, slid across skating rinks on his backside, joined the Army, unwillingly adopted an abandoned child, wistfully observed the gay happenings of Vanity Fair, survived policemen and bullies and bears and avalanches, tried to assuage his insatiable thirst for beautiful women, escaped into a world of unreality and was rudely shaken out of it; while men of all creeds and races and nations throughout the world gave themselves up to mirth, from the high-pitched giggle to the great guffaws of unrestrained belly laughter; while the years brought mankind from chaos through insecurity to disaster, the little tramp threw a gigantic shadow before him. It was the shadow of Charlie's silhouette, multiplied a thousandfold. For that one small figure showed himself increasingly to contain within him the loneliness and the fear, the desire to evade responsibility, the hopes and the pathos of the universal soul. Charlie, with his persistent battle for the individual spirit against the dragons and monsters of modern society that would defeat it, was heroic. His gentleness, his gallantry, his compassionate heart aching to enfold and protect those even weaker than himself, placed him among the great gentlemen of all time.

He became the quintessence of the undefeated. Their unyielding spirit shone in the little vagabond. Charlie—against whom every man's hand was turned, who had no place of his own upon this earth, for whom there was no love, nor any of the natural rights of man— Charlie was unconquerable. All the social cruelties and callousness of his day and age bewildered him; the great hand of destiny reached out to crush him between destructive greedy fingers. Charlie could not be crushed. And, even at the end when, as Verdoux, he was condemned to death, it was Society itself that was condemned. Even in death, Charlie triumphed over his dragon; and in so doing won a notable victory over everything that seeks to enslave and debase the human spirit.

Charlie seemed a puny David; but the potency of his weapons of satire and ridicule were shown by the howls of rage and pain and fear that came from the Goliaths he attacked. Charlie never changed, only expressed himself more clearly, more pungently, grew increasingly to the stature of a colossus.

Charlie is kin to all the heroes of mythology, and shares their unalterable destiny; but he is twin brother to Don Quixote, that knight of the sad countenance. The shabby knight is the shabby tramp, and both have elegance. In both burns the same fire of chivalry, both set forth on the same quest for the ideal, both built for themselves fantastic worlds nearer the ideal than reality could ever come. In both, truth and candour, gentleness and compassion dwelt side by side with inflexibility of will and purpose. Only Don Quixote was not so lonely. Rosinante and Sancho Panza, in their different ways, offered him fellowship. Charlie pursued his quest alone, unloved, sustained only by the intensity of his inner life.

Even when the establishment of talkies forced him into speech, the demand for Charlie was still universal—*Monsieur Verdoux* was given a special sound track in Hindustani; the dubbing was undertaken by a company in South Africa, and after its release in that country, the translation was shown in India. But before these complexities were made necessary, Charlie had spoken to white and black and yellow and red men in the universal language of comedy and pathos. He spoke to all mankind with the least gesture of his miraculous hands, the lift of an eyebrow, the droop of a shoulder. He spoke with his little cane and his large boots, with the white mask of his Pierrot face, and his eloquent eyes. In his silence, he spoke directly to each and every man, and allowed him to translate into his own tongue, against his own national background, the great basic truths of humankind that he presented to them. Charlie was never more eloquent than when he uttered no word, never funnier than when he suffered in silence the slings and arrows of outrageous fortune.

✍ Man of Many Talents

SO FABULOUS A CREATION AS CHARLIE IMPLIES A CREATOR OUT OF the ordinary, gifted with extraordinary talents. Chaplin's strength, and therefore Charlie's, lies in the fact that his genius has shown itself in multiple form, so that each of his films is entirely the result of his own creative impetus, and attains therefore an homogeneity denied to all other films.

Chaplin is a superlative mime; words have never been necessary to his work, and he alone of all the pioneers of film made no attempt to reproduce the verbal technique of the stage when he entered films. Mime is among the most ancient of the arts, and Chaplin the present master of it. May Reeves, among others, has instanced his gift, as when he acted for her benefit an unfortunate hunt with the Duke of Westminster. So vividly did he present the horrors of that chase that she saw him clearly in the hunting kit that was too large for him—the hunting pink with its tails trailing on the ground, the cuffs falling over his small hands, his waistcoat flapping over a lean stomach, and head gear that covered his eyes, and folded his ears in two. He could only just ride, and the horse took advantage of him. So wonderfully did he mime the scene that it was as though she were watching one of his films.

His Pierrot mask is more expressive in its immobility than the most frenzied contortions of the ham actor. In his mime and in his acting, Chaplin shows a subtlety, a technique, a sensitiveness that are without parallel.

As a dancer, he enters the highest ranks. No one with knowledge of dancing and choreography who has seen Chaplin move would deny him his place among the great ones; and most people who have met him or worked with him have noted what Martha Raye calls "his exquisite ballet-dancer gait".

Mime, actor, dancer blend into a comedian who ranges from grossest farce to most delicate satire, that is burnished with tears and loaded with grief even while it compels the heartiest laughter. As if they were flickering along through the old Bioscope, visions come crowding fast, and the ghost of past laughter is in the air—Charlie, in *Mabel's Strange Predicament* (1914), with the backward slant of the very tipsy, trying to conquer a staircase; his epic struggle with a folding wall bed possessed of a daemon in *One A.M.* (1916); his appearance in animal skin and bowler in *His Prehistoric Past* (1914), the hilarious prize fight in *The Champion* (1916), the riotous happenings on the farm in *The Tramp* (1915). Even the increasing satire and tragedy of his films could not check the ebullience of his comedy. *Shoulder Arms*

(1918), which told the bitter truth about war was nevertheless the film which had, among many others, the brilliant gag of the submerged head resting on the submerged pillow in the flooded dug-out. *The Circus* (1926), one of Chaplin's saddest films, contained some of his happiest comedy—the tightrope walk complicated by monkeys, the chase through the gallery of distorting mirrors; while all the Hynkel part of *The Great Dictator* (1940) makes full use of Chaplin's endless capacity for comic invention. Every film brings with it the memory of great comedy, of spent laughter.

Chaplin the interpretative artist comes then to his work loaded with more gifts in four different categories of expression—mime, acting, dancing and comedy—than most men have in any one of them; and that would be enough to secure him a memorable place in the world of entertainment.

His abundant creative vitality overflows. Charlie, expressing his poetic and philosophic self through the highly skilled interpretative gifts of his creator, is given still greater scope through the fact that he is produced, directed, edited, and later given musical accompaniment by that same Chaplin who first engendered him, then interpreted him, and finally controlled the whole of his expression and the medium in which he was expressed. Chaplin is very nearly as fabulous as Charlie.

The singlehearted purpose, the desire to have his work come whole and entire from his own hands and brain, the devotion and patience of the artist were shown by Chaplin when the coming of talking films caused him most furiously to think while he was making *City Lights* (1931) and to decide that the film must have a musical sound-track accompaniment. He was an accomplished executant; for three months he studied the composer's craft, and when he had mastered it, he composed the music for his completed film. He himself conducted the orchestra which played the music, so that *City Lights,* in spite of its unusual addition, was still Chaplin's whole work.

Chaplin the creator of Charlie is as fabulous an artist as his creation would lead us to suppose—indeed, Alexander Woolcott, in his lyrical appreciation of *City Lights,* goes so far as to say, "I would be prepared to defend the proposition that this darling of the mob is the foremost living artist".

His superb cinematic imagination is betrayed in everything he does, and certainly in his writing.* His book, *My Wonderful Visit,* written in a clipped nervous style, intensely personal, suddenly brings home the atmosphere of places and things, as when he describes the mystery of Limehouse at dusk—"There is a tang of the east in the air, living,

---

* See Appendix B.

moving, in this murky atmosphere, that is more intense even for the occasional dim light that peers out into the soft gloom from attic windows and storerooms, or municipal lights that gleam on the street corners. . . . And through it all, I have the feeling that things trivial, portentous, beautiful, sordid, cringing, glorious, simple, epochal, hateful, lovable are happening behind closed doors. I people all those shacks with girls, boys, murders, shrieks, life, beauty". Or the Thames waterside, the atmosphere of the Garrick Club, the physical aspects of poverty—the decayed and broken houses, the dirty littered streets, the little shops loaded with cheap goods. His alert eye selects, and his pen records the camera-worthy angles of everything he sees. All this illuminates a statement he once made to H. G. Wells: "The only way I notice things is on the run. Whatever keenness of perception I have is momentary, fleeting. I observe all in ten minutes, or not at all"; and explains too the imaginative detail of all his films.

Everything in him marks the artist, and nothing more than his endless quest for perfection, his inability ever to be satisfied with the results of his wholehearted, sensitive, meticulous work. Each film completed becomes for him only the stepping stone to the next; and Chaplin's severest critic has been more lenient to his work than he has ever been himself.

Beneath the specific expressions of his artistry—mime, acting, dancing, the making of films—is to be found the poet and the musician. Sam Goldwyn has said of him, "He is a poet—the great poet of the screen. His fierce rebellions against man-made fetters, which would trammel the individual soul in its progress towards complete expression, his sensitiveness to impression, his combination of emotionality and complete detachment—these ally him in spirit with the youngest and fieriest of bards".

The musician, so closely akin to the poet, is present in Chaplin. He has made a prolonged study of this other art, until now he has mastered the violin, the 'cello, the organ; and is able to compose his own film music, and conduct its orchestration. Chaplin's energy is protean, and impels him to lead the lives of many artists, creative and interpretative, in his unique person.

✑ Chaplin at Work

MAX LINDER, WHOSE OWN INCOMPARABLE WORK IN THE EARLY DAYS of French film delighted Chaplin, gave the latter a full accolade as early as 1919 when he wrote, "It is impossible to get any idea of the continuous and highly intelligent effort of Charlie Chaplin in his work. He calls me his teacher, but, for my part, I have been lucky to get lessons at his school. He works for the camera with the minutest care".

Linder, a great artist himself, was quick to perceive and commend in the young Chaplin a constant preoccupation with perfection. Already at that time, only four years after he had entered films, he was proving himself an able and imaginative producer, so that, again according to Linder, "from first to last, spectators of every race, and of every type of mind, could follow the evolution of his thought and the very finest touches of his wit".

To this testimony, one of his early secretaries, Elsie Codd, added amusing detail—of days and nights of bad temper, during what she called the "incubation period", which began when some comic incident in real life had inspired him to start thinking about a new film. After this brooding period, which sometimes took him off alone to Catalina Island, he would expound his ideas to a few chosen friends, using their comments as a stimulus to further ideas. Once the theme had grown clear and fixed, there was no more delay or solitude. The film once started, all was fire and fury, endless patience and concentration, until it was done.

Chaplin on the job was from the beginning absolute master of every detail. Each member of his company, dressed and made-up, was inspected by him before the day's shooting began. Each scene was described in detail, with a joyousness and vitality that made working with him, in spite of, or perhaps because of, his determined search for perfection, an enjoyment and a unique experience. In the early days, a super of considerable experience said of him, "He is so kind and patient, and above all he's so different somehow"; while Martha Raye, who took part in *Monsieur Verdoux* (1947) said that to work with an artist like Chaplin was not only an honour and a privilege, but enormous fun. "For us all, Charlie is the tops!"

The scene once explained, the players rehearsed their parts endlessly, Chaplin having interpreted every single rôle, to such a degree that Miss Codd is able to state "without exaggeration, I think I can say that he has played every character in every one of his comedies".

Throughout the whole rehearsal period, Chaplin's unflagging vitality and enthusiasm whipped his players into an excitement that made them give of their best. He was himself a protean figure, now an old gent puffing along in anger, now a simple maiden bowed in grief, now a masher swaggering into a park, now the harassed mother of many children; always building the compact lines of his perfect comedies, dovetailing cause and effect, paring down to essentials, inventing the most fantastic comedy gags, sweeping everyone before him into the fanatical blaze of his unleashed creative power, and his unbounded energy.

When, after exhausting and exhilarating repetitions, his exacting standards were as nearly satisfied as they could ever be, Chaplin the producer was transformed into Chaplin the director, who gave to the camera the same meticulous attention the other had given to rehearsing the scene. Sometimes, in those early days of improvisation, he would think of a new idea when the camera had finished shooting, rehearse and record it immediately, while inspiration was at fever heat within him.

Every morning, Chaplin began by seeing the previous day's work, noting the comparative merits of the variations on a single theme, so that later, as he built and cut his film, a spool the length of a whole comedy would be reduced to a minute's showing time .

Nor did his preoccupation with every aspect of his work end in the studio. He has described the way in which he finds himself continually observing people, and watching their reactions, relative to his films—"When I am watching one of my own films at a public performance, I keep one eye on the screen, and the other and my two ears on the spectators. I notice what makes them laugh and what does not. If, for example, at several performances the public does not laugh at some touch which I meant to be funny, I at once set to work to find what was wrong with the idea or its execution, or perhaps with the process of photographing it. And very often I notice a little laugh from some gesture which was not studied, and then I prick up my ears, and try to find out why this particular point has made them laugh. In a way, when I go to see one of my films I am like a tradesman watching what his customers are carrying or buying or doing. And just as I observe the public in a theatre to see what makes it laugh, so I observe it to find ideas for comic scenes."

Chaplin has taken into the complex machinery of modern film-making all his artist's integrity. Now and then, his collaborators find themselves back in the early days of film making, for Chaplin is autocratic in his work, and if it pleases him to introduce elements from the Keystone days into his latest films, or make use of outmoded technique, no one would care to oppose him. His anger is terrible when his decisions are questioned; but he is capable of sober reflection after an outburst, and of finally accepting a tentative suggestion, if he afterwards realizes that it is better than his own.

The impetus of Chaplin's attack upon his work astounds the people who work with him. He demands everything from them, exhausts them, but himself works harder, and for longer hours, than even his most devoted henchman. While he is working on a film, his nerves are stretched to breaking point, and he is tensed to such a pitch that all his technicians work twice as hard and twice as fast as they had believed possible.

Chaplin detests the apparatus of his medium—the cameras, the microphone, the lights, the travelling stages, accepting them balefully as necessary evils, but giving all his interest to the rehearsal of the takes, and driving his continuity-girl into near insanity with his blithe indifference to the need for exact repetition of detail in consecutive shots. To this day, he first takes the scenes that appeal to him particularly, going haphazardly from set to set, and increasing the burdens of his script and continuity girls and his associate producers until only his integrity and his charm save him from rebellion or desertion.

When the moment for shooting has come, he is wholly absorbed, his pockets crammed with last-minute ideas, gags, changes in décor scribbled on odd scraps of paper through the wakeful hours of the night; first at the studio, and last to leave it, sometimes never leaving it for days on end.

Side by side with the volcanic Chaplin entirely taken up with his work goes the amusing fellow-worker of the old days. He is still capable, in a moment's pause between scenes, of launching into vivid impersonations, impassioned dramatic scenes, a piano concerto or a little light fooling, so that the executives who a moment before were breathing fire and fury before the erratic demands made upon them, relax under the magic of the Chaplin who had known how to hold crowds enthralled.

As soon, however, as the next scene is prepared, the momentary relaxation is immediately cut short, and Chaplin plunges into work again with the same ardour and the same fury, taking a scene twenty, thirty, forty times, until it approaches his requirements.

In spite of his apparently erratic methods, his refusal to save time by shooting scenes in sequence, his insistence on long rehearsal periods, and multiple takes for every shot, Chaplin can complete a film in minimum time if he chooses—*Monsieur Verdoux* took exactly twelve weeks, and no one in Hollywood who knew his methods would believe it. This in itself is proof that Chaplin is always master of the chaos into which he plunges his studios while he is on the job.

Dressed like a tramp, driving himself in a battered Ford, tearing like a whirlwind through the studios, Chaplin invariably brings his chosen rabbit out of the hat. He tends to spend an increasing length of time over the preparation of his films. When he had bought out Orson Welles over the Verdoux theme, he spent four years over the writing of the scenario, brooding over it, leaving it for a while; returning to it with renewed eagerness, determined to give the scenario all the time it required for its development. There is never anything hasty or unfinished in any part of Chaplin's work, in spite of his impetuousness.

His contribution to film is immeasurable. Of the pioneers in America, he was the first true creator in the new medium; and the only one to apply, from the beginning, film technique to film craft. In the earliest films, he stands out as the only player who did not open and shut his mouth in what seemed a silent parody of human speech, who did not use extravagant and uncontrolled gesture to express emotion, as did all the others. Chaplin used his face and his body, all its movement, and its stillness, to express his character in terms of pure film. He set about his own independent voyage of discovery, and moulded his medium according to the exigencies of his creative expression. Because of his initially right approach, he was the creator of his art, and invented the form it took. With him, silent film reached its peak.

A clock taken to pieces is not a clock and does not go; a ballet analysed in terms of décor, costume, music, choreography is neither a ballet nor an æsthetic experience. So a book that analyses a legendary figure and its creator tends to destroy their essential quality. The danger is that he who takes the clock to pieces cannot put it together again; he who takes Charlie to pieces to find out what makes him go may lose sight of the whole creation. Yet Charlie is, however handled, indestructible; and able to pick up the pieces himself, through the irresistible force of his own personality, and the affection and memories of the millions who grew up with him.

✍ His Lasting Fame

TWENTY YEARS AGO, EMIL LUDWIG, THE WELL-KNOWN PUBLICIST and author, interviewed Chaplin for the Viennese newspaper, *Neue Freie Presse*. He was immediately struck with Chaplin's air of tranquillity, which he had not expected, since Chaplin had never shown any signs before of that inner calm which brings with it a tranquil presence; and then by his mental quality.

For Ludwig, part of Chaplin's fascination lay in the fact that here was a poor boy who became a millionaire through playing one rôle only, that of a down-at-heel tramp; another part expressed itself in terms of rhetoric—"What is the fame of Gandhi compared with him who has shaken the world as only the figure of Christ has done before him? There is no one yet who has sustained such world-wide fame, and yet remains so simple and unaffected".

These are large claims: yet it is certain that Chaplin's universal appeal, together with his overwhelming artistry, explain the deep and abiding interest he has aroused among all manner of people over the face of the earth. He once said of himself: "Ideally, I am a disciple of Anatole France, rather than one of Bernard Shaw. Where Shaw is an ethical teacher, Anatole France philosophically knows nothing of good or bad, much the same as myself. As for ideals, they are dangerous playthings, barren of results, and for the most part, false." The amoral quality in Chaplin, and through him in Charlie, did not outlast the early years. It is interesting, moreover, that the man who found ideals dangerous and barren has in all his films presented an ideal of human conduct, through satirizing its reverse; and, what is still more important, has endeared himself to millions through his idealist-tramp Charlie.

Chaplin's position in the world has from the beginning been unique. On the one hand he is loved, adored, fêted, idolized, publicized, photographed, mobbed by wholehearted admirers all over the world. All the Allied trenches in the 1914-18 war rang to the songs the Tommies sang about him. He rose from poverty to fabulous wealth, from obscure origins to an entrée into every social milieu, fêted by the distinguished people of his time. On the other hand, Chaplin is featured in every scurrility that could be printed about him, attacked and vilified by all those he seemed to pillory in his astounding work, howled down for his morals, his politics, and above all, his unbreakable individuality.

It would have been small wonder if he had lost his head under the strain of maintaining normal balance on such a see-saw, and shown in his life and work an increasing deterioration. Yet the reverse has been true; and one of the major interests of any study of Chaplin must be in the integration and full flowering of his personality and genius over the years.

In 1942, seventeen years after it had been voted the best film of 1925, the *Gold Rush* was reissued. A few scenes were cut, a few previously unused replaced them; and Chaplin composed a musical score and substituted a commentary spoken by himself for the old subtitles.

The reissue proved that Charlie is timeless, ageless, a great clown and a superlative mime. Where normally the release of old films causes laughter at their oddness, the *Gold Rush* compelled that same tribute of laughter and tears and a choke in the throat that another generation had offered to it seventeen years before. In Paris, where the film was also shown, Charlot became a symbol of the resistance movement, an embodiment of the unconquerable spirit of mankind.

Recently, *City Lights* has been reissued, with the same result. In a world caught up in a struggle on the one side anarchic—the struggle of the individual to put his ego above society; and on the other side materialist—the struggle to put society above the individual, a world confused and exhausted, living on nerves stretched to breaking point, Charlie comes as a release and a solace, paradoxically enough, since he is himself part of the struggle. Long queues have stretched round cinemas, waiting even in the rain to see, not the latest Hollywood stupendous, but a delicate film made twenty years ago, a silent film that went straight to the heart; and goes still to the unchanging heart of the people everywhere.

No other maker of films has been able to cross the frontiers of time as Chaplin has; nor is this his only immortality. He has been received among the hierarchy of clowns, has joined the immortal family of the world of entertainment.

For there have been clowns since man first recognized in himself and his neighbour the impulse to laugh cruelly at deformity. They were already present in the circuses and public spectacles of Ancient Egypt, Rome and Greece. Through the centuries, their paths crossed those of the Commedia dell 'Arte, harlequinade and pantomime. The savagery of the laughter they had first aroused gave place to affection; what had originally been natural deformity became assumed grotesqueness, until, with the development of the modern circus, came its own family of clowns, of the highest pedigree, if not of unbroken line.

First comes the *entrée* clown, superb in spangles and frill, born and bred in the Big Top; then the *auguste,* reaching back into the past as far as Augustus Cæsar, to a progenitor savage and monstrous, alive with political satire and the crude malice of barbarians, but now a fantastic figure of fun, forever doomed to be too tall or too short, too slow or too quick, prone to stumble, to receive pails of water in the face, to slip over a banana skin, forever to blunder and to fail, and be taken to the warm hearts of children, who, watching him fall flat upon his face as he enters the ring, shout with the welcome given only to the dearest friends "Auguste idiot!". To these aristocrats of the circus was added the *Joey,* based on the tradition, costume and make-up of Joseph Grimaldi, one of the most famous clowns of harlequinade in the eighteenth and early nineteenth century.

Now, in our own time, and in his own time, comes the *Charlie,* so that throughout the world, wherever circuses put up their mushroom growths for a few nights or a few weeks, and the clowns, augustes and Joeys tumble into the ring, each in his traditional costume, there will be found the baggy trousers, huge boots, little bowler, cane, and moustache, of the *Charlie.*

All circus clowns have their special tradition and technique, in many cases handed down from father to son; and it is interesting to note, in view of its derivation, that the *Charlie* is a "wonderfully effective combination of the dumbshow actor, the comedian and the circus clown who performs as an acrobat or juggler. The cleverest *Charlie* to-day is Charles Rivels, one of the highest paid clowns in the circus ring".

So Charlie the little tramp, who is perhaps the greatest clown the world has ever known, in the widest sense of the term, is also a member of the most exclusive fraternity of circus clowns, the first since Grimaldi, who died in 1837.

Charlie has a warm and perpetual throne, and his accession to it is demonstrated in a million incidents like this one: Two children, Susan and Caroline, who know little of world chaos, the burdens of adult humanity, the solitude and sadness that weigh upon the spirit; nothing of Chaplin's loneliness, nor of his consummate art, nothing of his quest after his Holy Grail—these two watched some of Chaplin's early films, for the first time in their lives, at a party, and rolled upon the floor, and choked in an ecstasy of joy and laughter, ached and gasped and groaned with laughter; wept for him; and loved him.

When Chaplin's detractors have all come to ignominious dust, together with the fragile film that holds all that is mortal of the greatest clown, the *Charlie* will still bring a shout of recognition and joy from the circus arena, increasing and maintaining the legendary and lovable quality of the little tramp, securing his immortality. While, so long as Chaplin's generation walks the earth, the *Charlie* will bring with him nostalgic memories of the unconquerable little tramp, with his tight jacket and baggy trousers, small bowler and large boots, forever setting out along an endless road, seeking eternally with all the ardour of his great and candid soul, a perfection always out of reach.

APPENDICES

APPENDIX A

The Films of Charles Chaplin

RELEASE DATES GIVEN

1914—*The Keystone Films*. With Chester Conklin, Alice Davenport, Henry Lehrman, Minta Durfee, the Keystone Kids, Mabel Normand, Harry McCoy, Hank Mann, Ford Sterling, Fatty Arbuckle, Mack Sennett, Edgar Kennedy, Mack Swain, Charles Murray, Slim Summerville, Charley Chase, the Keystone Cops, Al St. John, etc.

FEBRUARY	*Making A Living* (1 reel)
	Kid Auto Races at Venice (split reel)
	Mabel's Strange Predicament (1 reel)
	Between Showers (1 reel)
MARCH	*A Film Johnnie* (1 reel)
	Tango Tangles (1 reel)
	His Favourite Pastime (1 reel)
	Cruel, Cruel Love (1 reel)
APRIL	*The Star Boarder* (1 reel)
	Mabel at the Wheel (2 reels)
	Twenty Minutes Of Love (1 reel)
	Caught in a Cabaret (2 reels)
MAY	*Caught in the Rain* (1 reel)
	A Busy Day (split reel)
JUNE	*The Fatal Mallet* (1 reel)
	Her Friend the Bandit (1 reel)
	The Knockout (2 reels)
	Mabel's Busy Day (1 reel)
	Mabel's Married Life (1 reel)
JULY	*Laughing Gas* (1 reel)
AUGUST	*The Property Man* (2 reels)
	The Face on the Barroom Floor (1 reel)
	Recreation (split reel)
	The Masquerader (1 reel)
	His New Profession (1 reel)
SEPTEMBER	*The Bounders* (1 reel)
	The New Janitor (1 reel)

OCTOBER	*Those Love Pangs* (1 reel)
	Dough and Dynamite (2 reels)
	Gentlemen of Nerve (1 reel)
NOVEMBER	*His Musical Career* (1 reel)
	His Trysting Place (2 reels)
	Tillie's Punctured Romance (6 reels)
	(cast included Marie Dressler)
DECEMBER	*Getting Acquainted* (1 reel)
	His Prehistoric Past (2 reels)

These are slapstick comedies in the Karno-Sennett tradition, with Charlie emerging. His mannerisms are evolved, his fastidiousness, his troubles with inanimate objects and with incongruous situations. Noteworthy are his acrobatic qualities, his dancing; and the fact that his first feature-length comedy, *Tillie's Punctured Romance,* was made in this first year.

1915—*The Essanay Films.* With Ben Turpin, Leo White, Edna Purviance, Bud Jamison, Lloyd Bacon, Billy Armstrong, Paddy McGuire, Marta Golden, Wesley Ruggles, etc.

FEBRUARY	*His New Job* (2 reels)
	A Night Out (2 reels)
MARCH	*The Champion* (2 reels)

Remarkable for its analogies to ballet. The development of the story, its timing, and its use of movement, shape and rhythm are all choreographic. The scenes in the training quarters (where punch ball, dumb bells, Indian clubs and skipping rope are all endowed with malevolent life), in the ring, and during the fight itself, are all dancing scenes.

The film opens with Charlie sharing with his pet bulldog his last frankfurter, which the dog refuses to eat until Charlie has put salt upon it. The acting of this and subsequent scenes is impeccable —Charlie's absorption in the grave business of sharing the food, and making it palatable to the dog, his search for the salt which must be taken daintily from the recesses of his pockets and sprinkled with elegance over the rejected article; his coxcomb showing-off to the fair lady (Edna Purviance); his highly dramatic and burlesqued farewell to his dog before he goes to fight—all this has the authentic subtlety of Charlie's best mime, in which the flick of an eyebrow and the play of a little finger are more eloquent than speech.

In the Park (1 reel)

APRIL	*The Jitney Elopement* (2 reels)
	The Tramp (2 reels)

Here for the first time is an undercurrent of pathos; the first appearance of the outcast, the wanderer without shelter. From the opening scene of the limitless dusty road bordered with stunted bushes, and the little defenceless figure walking wearily down it towards the cameras, constantly bowled over and left in the dust by motors speeding past, the note of solitude and pathos is set; and at the end of the film we have for the first time that poignant finish when Charlie, once more defeated in his search for love, a roof, a place of his own in the world, walks sadly away down the long road and then, inveterate optimist, adventurous vagabond, shrugs away sadness, kicks up his heels, and waddles eagerly towards the horizon.

There are wonderful touches that bring to light the essential fastidiousness, the dandyism of the shabby tramp. Bowled over by cars, rolled in the dust, he is no sooner upon his feet again than out comes a whisk brush from the recesses of his person; and with infinite care he brushes himself down, shoots his cuffs, settles his bowler, rubs up his boots on the backs of his trouser legs and meets his next encounter with a car like a gentleman. The dandy is apparent again as he prepares to eat by the wayside by dipping his fingers into water, and cleaning his nails with a knife, all this with a sober unselfconsciousness. The Don Quixote is there, when Charlie rescues the fair maiden from thieves; and the eternal little fellow filled with a desire to love and be loved. Here diabolic life is given to objects, so that loaded sacks and pitchforks and eggs, with irresistible comedy, become instruments of the fate dogging the steps of the outcast.

	By the Sea (1 reel)
JUNE	*Work* (2 reels)
JULY	*A Woman* (2 reels)
AUGUST	*The Bank* (2 reels)

Offers ample evidence of the further development of Chaplin's original line, and a reiteration of the pathetic element in the little tramp. This film is a microcosm of Chaplin's work, and on that count extremely valuable as an historic document, as well as for its own sake as a remarkably perfect work of art. The opening shot makes wonderful use of the humour of incongruity, when Charlie enters an imposing bank, opens with great dignity an enormous vault—and brings out a mop and pail, becoming at once the janitor. Objects enter into the persecution against him—the mop achieves a violent life of its own that involves him disastrously with other people; alight with passionate love and ecstasy he blows a kiss to the beloved he worships from afar, turns and immediately bumps into a door. In this film too, Charlie is doomed to love in vain. His pathetic flowers are despised and rejected, his fervent note torn up. There is an unforgettable close-up of Charlie, watching his beloved's reaction to his gift through a keyhole, fingers pressed to his mouth in excitement, like a child at a party. As he sees his gift scornfully rejected, the same pose turns into a mask of sadness and the fingers droop from his mouth in utter desolation. It would be impossible to analyse the subtle and complex means by which the excited child, retaining the same pose, becomes the desolate unwanted. The result is profoundly moving: humanity recognizing its essential loneliness.

Here too for the first time is the use of a dream sequence, transporting Charlie to a world of fantasy in which he is admired, respected, loved, a dynamic hero incapable of blunder. Only to find a cruel awakening expressed in the shots in which Charlie on the verge of embracing his love, is replaced by Charlie fervently embracing his mop. The fine dream is faded, reality oppresses him again. And as in *The Tramp*, he walked lonely down the endless road, so now, with the same weary resignation and the same unquenchable optimism, he wanders back to the vault.

OCTOBER	*Shanghaied* (2 reels)
NOVEMBER	*A Night in the Show* (2 reels)
1916—APRIL	*Carmen* (4 reels)

A burlesque of the Cecil B. de Mille film of the opera.

MARCH	*Police* (2 reels)
1918—AUGUST	*Triple Trouble* (2 reels)

1916-1917—*The Mutual Films*. With Edna Purviance, Eric Campbell, Lloyd Bacon, Charlotte Mineau, Leo White, John Rand, Frank J. Coleman, James T. Kelley, Albert Austin, Henry Bergman, etc.

MAY	*The Floorwalker* (2 reels)
JUNE	*The Fireman* (2 reels)
JULY	*The Vagabond* (2 reels)
AUGUST	*One A.M.* (2 reels)

An example of Chaplin's experimental approach to cinema at this time. The theme of the film is of the slightest—Charlie returning home drunk after a convivial evening, trying to get upstairs and into bed; and its virtuosity lies in the fact that Charlie is the sole actor, apart from the taxi driver in the opening shots. Here he gives full rein to his particular and fantastic use of properties. A car door, a tiger-skin rug, a stuffed animal, a staircase, and, above all, a folding bed, become his fellow actors, the source of his misfortunes, the instruments of implacable destiny. Once again, the film is essentially ballet, a solo by a male dancer of the highest order, a Nijinski of drunkenness.

His struggle with the unmanageable bed is not only physical, but taken to a mental plane, when every reaction to the monster is reflected on his amazed, shocked, hurt and angry face. The film possesses the curiously poetic element that shines forth from all his work—for while Charlie stumbles, falls, slips, glides, dances and struggles, he conveys, as no one else has ever been able to do, the curious kingdom into which a drunken man enters, his inviolability there, where even those things most hostile to him fail to impinge upon him, where everything has its own, indifferent reality. In this case, the bed wins and will not be slept in! Yet the last victory is with Charlie, who sinks into the innocent and profound sleep of a child, in the bath, crowned with his defiant topper!

SEPTEMBER   *The Count* (2 reels)
               (contains an original tango by Chaplin)

OCTOBER   *The Pawnshop* (2 reels)

The subtlest of this series, with a perfection of rhythm and shape that are outstanding among all Chaplin's films up to this date. The characters in this film are far more than types; their relations with, and reactions to, Charlie, are an integral part of the comedy. Chaplin's best mime is to be found in this film; and his power to breathe life into inanimate objects has never been more ably demonstrated. This element of magic, of something more than ordinary life lived at ordinary levels, pervades the whole film, reaching its apotheosis in the scene in which Charlie, utterly absorbed, deeply serious, reduces an alarm clock to its smallest component parts. His busy fingers—and how wonderfully expressive they are!—attack the clock, while his face expresses not only the emotions and reactions proper to each separate craftsman but an over-all absorption like that of a child entirely given over to one special miracle in a world of miracles. His final gesture of negation and renunciation as he throws the useles pieces into the hat of his astonished customer, washing his hands literally and metaphorically of the chaos he has wrought, fixing him with cold, clear eyes that dare him to question or to comment, is a masterpiece all by itself.

NOVEMBER *Behind the Screen* (2 reels)

DECEMBER *The Rink* (2 reels)
Contains a very beautiful waltz on skates.

1917—JANUARY *Easy Street* (2 reels)

APRIL *The Cure* (2 reels)

JUNE *The Immigrant* (2 reels)
Noteworthy—the superb irony of that shot in which the refugees, packed like sardines on board ship, are roped in by the ship's officials at the very moment they catch sight of the Statue of Liberty.

OCTOBER *The Adventurer* (2 reels)

1918-1922—*The First National Films.* With Edna Purviance, Chuck Reisner, Henry Bergman, Albert Austin, Syd Chaplin, Tom Wilson, Jackie Coogan, Mack Swain, etc.

APRIL *A Dog's Life* (3 reels)
Packed with comedy and pathos. Realism due to autobiographical factors.

AUGUST *The Bond* (half reel)
Propaganda film made for the Liberty Loan Committee.

OCTOBER *Shoulder Arms* (3 reels)
The perfect expression of Chaplin's genius. Artistically it offers the best of Chaplin—pace, rhythm, comedy, burlesque, satire, pathos, and brilliant mime. Charlie at war is still Charlie, taken from one dog's life into another. The lovely comedy of his attempt to sleep in the flooded dug-out, when he is forced at last to put his head under the water in order to lay it upon his submerged pillow; his attempt to blow out his candle floating upon the water—attempts that send it sailing under the bare feet of his neighbouring bedfellows; the hilarious scene in which he disguises himself as a tree—oh shades of Dunsinane!—and knocks out Germans who come to gather him for firewood—all these offer Charlie at his comic best. But there is pathos too. Who can ever forget the stab at the heart that came with the sight of the little soldier nibbling cheese from the mouse-trap? He alone had received no parcel of food from home, so he pretended to enjoy the cheese, refusing friendly offers to share with the fixed, forced smile that hides loneliness and neglect and pride.

Remember him reading, with a passionate interest and excitement and appreciation, other people's letters from home, over their hostile shoulders, because he had none himself. Wordlessly, soundlessly, with mime so subtle it defies analysis, so brilliant it defies description, Chaplin limns in his masterpiece—the little soldier, outcast still and lonely, caught up in the jaws of Moloch, suffering the true rigors of war—the boredom, the desolation, the lost hours and days and years, the cessation of living, and the familiarity of death. Is it any wonder that the trenches rang with the name of "Charlie"?

1919—JUNE   *Sunnyside* (3 reels)
Here Chaplin the poet reaches his full development and gives himself wholly to the lyrical element that has crept imperceptibly into his work. Once more, as with *The Champion,* and *One A.M.,* the film is balletic in composition, and dancing plays an actual part in it, as does the dream sequence idea first to be found in *The Bank.*

In spite of its comedy and burlesque, *Sunnyside* is unique among all Chaplin's films for its highly developed poetic quality. It is a lyric. Two sequences stand out particularly, and for opposite reasons. One, the scenes with the nymphs in the dream, where Chaplin's superlative dancing overcomes the initial disadvantages of baggy trousers, tight waistcoat and shirt sleeves, to achieve, in spite of them, a miracle of beauty, the purest poetry of motion; and the utterly ridiculous sequence in which, having lost his cows, he takes the head of a yokel between his hands and stares long and hard at him, as though to make quite sure, in his own mind, that this is not one of the missing beasts. The eager, searching look, its blend of hope and disappointment, is unforgettable.

1919—DECEMBER   *A Day's Pleasure* (2 reels)

1921—FEBRUARY   *The Kid* (6 reels)
Charlie's motherly care of his adopted baby, his instilling of standards of behaviour, their manner of living, is comedy touched with tears. His fight to save his "kid" from the hands of officialdom, austerely stretched out to take him to frigid safety, leave the tears with no comedy to dry them. The ensuing battle to rear the child himself, without the interference of cruel philanthropy, is an epic blend of comedy and tragedy, where Charlie's well-known indomitable spirit reaches new heights of endurance.

There is burlesque too; but even burlesque, in the hands of this incomparable master, undergoes a strange metamorphosis, and approaches poetry. The famous dream sequence of *The Kid* is an example of this.

1921—SEPTEMBER *The Idle Class* (2 reels)

1922—APRIL *Pay Day* (2 reels)

1923—FEBRUARY *The Pilgrim* (4 reels)

The initial irony of Charlie's escape from prison in the garb of a minister of God sets the tone of the film and gives full scope to its satirical intention, carried out with a lightness of touch that in no way minimises the cruelty of its ridicule. Two sequences stand out with memorable clarity. One is the sermon on David and Goliath in which Charlie, mainly through his expressive hands, creates for his audience—his congregation—a clear and vivid vision of the Biblical story. It is surely not by chance that that particular story was chosen. For Charlie himself is a David in arms against the Goliath of Society and the myrmidons of Society—the Church, the State, and the Law; and we are irresistibly reminded of this as we watch the extraordinary pantomimic skill of Charlie the convict disguised as a minister. Through the film is the glowing comedy of Charlie's adaptability to the new rôle thrust upon him, together with certain lapses from it, as when he hangs upon the bars of a ticket-office grille much as a convict hangs upon the bars of his cell.

The final sequence of *The Pilgrim* tends also to be remembered where much else is forgotten. It is in some measure the summing up not only of the film, but of Charlie's whole philosophy of life. Led to the frontier of Mexico by a well-intentioned sheriff who wishes to save him from a return to prison, Charlie is about to escape joyously into freedom, when gunshots testify to the presence of bandits on the Mexican border. Charlie is on the horns of a dilemma. On the one side of the frontier—prison; on the other—mortal danger. So Charlie runs steadily along the frontier, one foot in America, one in Mexico, daring fate to do its worst, and prudently postponing his final choice. This is perhaps the most enjoyable ending of any of Chaplin's films, and one that is typically significant.

1923-1947—*United Artists Films*.

1923—*A Woman of Paris* (8 reels). Released 1st October.
> Cast: Edna Purviance, Adolphe Menjou, Carl Miller, Lydia Knott, Charles French, Clarence Geldert, Betty Morrissey, Malvina Polo, Nelly Bly Baker.

The opening shot of the film creates its atmosphere. Night, silence, and sadness expressed by a few roof-tops, a wall, a lighted window. The beauty and originality of the film lay in its psychological subtlety and in its simplicity of construction; every effect is made through understatement.

The most striking example of this controlled simplicity is the classic scene of the departure of Marie St. Clair for Paris: it is an example too of the transcendental quality in Chaplin's work, which leaves us pursuing his thought on several different planes at once, a quality that makes his work as subtle and complex as thought itself.

The history of cinema to this date was studded with several scenes of departure stations, where the fullest use had been made of steam and light and shadow, the panting approach and dwindling exit of trains, the crowds and bustle, to symbolize parting or reunion or loss. Then Chaplin brought his genius to bear upon the well-known factors, and once more created the unforgettable in what was perhaps the first expressionistic use of his medium known to America. For here there is none of the plethora of realistic detail. Only the girl poised between light and shadow, quite still. Then the lights from an unseen train are projected upon her, slowing down, coming to a stop. And she comes forward, alone. There is no train, no station, no human being other than the girl. But through his masterly elimination, Chaplin conveys light, shadow and stillness—first the girl on the very brink of what we discover immediately afterwards to be the destruction of her integrity and the beginning of her tragedy. Then, there is the panic of being alone at night in darkness that is part of our ancient heritage of fear, that has its immediate application to the girl waiting on the brink of a precipice. With all this, such beauty of light and shadow and the dark, still girl that for this scene alone, cinema may rightly be termed an art, to rank with the highest. The feeling of the whole film is as sombre and doomladen as any Greek tragedy, a masterly accusation of puritanism, a denunciation of a shallow, elegant society that Chaplin had discovered to be without faith or heart. Being what they are, the characters must react as they do; and fate steps in at every turn to ensure their tragedy.

1925—*The Gold Rush* (9 reels). Released 16th August.

Cast: Charlie Chaplin, Mack Swain, Tom Murray, Georgia Hale, Betty Morrissey, Malcolm Waite, Henry Bergman

(*Re-issued April, 1942, with music and commentary by Chaplin*)

Perhaps Chaplin's most famous film. Contains several unforgettable shots—Charlie's lonely silhouette against the immense snows of Alaska—the episode of the stewed boots—the avalanche that carries his log cabin to the edge of the precipice and leaves it rocking over space.

The most poignant scenes are those of the party to which no one came, together with the dance of the rolls, which transcend all else.

Charlie, with infinite care and love, quivering with excitement, arranges a New Year's Eve party in his cabin for Georgia and her friends, and sits down to wait for them with the beaming face of an excited child. His waning excitement, his refusal to realize that they are not coming, together with his final acceptance of the fact, are of the same unendurable poignancy as the major part of *The Kid*, so that he becomes the living symbol of that isolation of the spirit that is beyond remedy. Waiting, and losing hope, he impales two rolls upon the prongs of two forks and makes them dance.

1928—*The Circus* (7 reels). Released 7th January.

Cast: Allan Garcia, Merna Kennedy, Betty Morrissey, Harry Crocker, Stanley Sanford, John Rand, George Davis, Henry Bergman, Steve Murphy, Doc Stone and Charlie Chaplin.

The film contains some of Chaplin's funniest comedy effects—his careless finger that inadvertently releases the catch of the magician's box of tricks, giving the show away and creating chaos—the tight rope act attended by a swarm of escaped monkeys who complicate his manœuvres—the death leap by bicycle that takes him out of the big top, out of the fairground into the middle of a hardware store. The last shot is noteworthy. As the caravans lumber away, taking with them the happy lovers, Charlie stands immobile, watching them recede into the distance. Nothing remains of the circus but the outline of the ring upon the turf and, at his feet, a piece of paper with a star on it, that once covered the hoop through which his beloved little equestrienne used to jump. Charlie holds it for a while, dreaming, desolate, despairing. Then, suddenly, with his special jaunty kick, he sends the paper flying, and off he goes, sadness in abeyance now, towards the horizon that endlessly promises adventure to the free soul.

1931—*City Lights* (87 minutes). Released 6th February.

Cast: Virginia Cherrill, Florence Lee, Harry Myers, Allan Garcia, Hank Mann and Charlie Chaplin.

Music composed by Charles Chaplin.

(Re-issued 1950).

The theme—of Charlie's gallant attempts to keep a roof over the head of the young blind flower-seller, his precarious friendship with the whimsical millionaire, with whom their fates become inextricably woven—gives Chaplin full scope for his peculiar gift of poignancy; and for expressing in terms of cinema the most delicate and subtle relationships, as he had already done in *A Woman of Paris* and *The Gold Rush*. Here, the relationship between Charlie and the flower-seller, spiritualized by her blindness and his chivalry, is miraculously sustained on a plane at once human and sublime, so that the cruelty of the final scenes impinge sharply. Charlie, dejected and alone, without his cane, recently released from prison, comes back to find her happily installed in her shop, her sight restored. She bursts out laughing at first sight of the funny down-at-heels little tramp staring so fixedly at her; then, ashamed, offers him a flower in apology, and some money, because he so obviously needs it. Their hands touch, and something of the extra sense remaining from her blindness tells her that here before her is her benefactor. "Yes, I can see now". The bitterest sub-title Chaplin ever used, and as tragic as the final shot of Charlie holding the flower and smiling at her with a terrified and poignant realization that reality has destroyed the illusion existing between them. Among the comedy effects, the incident of the penny whistle, where the feeble chirrup of the invisible article, swallowed inadvertently by Charlie when a boisterous girl slaps him on the chest, compels a laughter near hysteria. Fate never deals Charlie single blows. He gets hiccups and becomes a social pariah. His fellow guests are as embarrassed as he is; a singer, determined to show his prowess, cannot start, for his every beginning is marred by the faint cheep of the whistle as Charlie struggles with his hiccups. Alone in a garden, Charlie's invisible whistle calls a taxi; then some dogs, until Charlie returns to the party in despair at the head of a pack. These incidents, when the film was shown in Paris, drew the same hysterical laughter from a very cosmopolitan group of students, of most races, most nations.

1936—*Modern Times* (85 minutes). Released 5th February.

> Cast: Paulette Goddard, Henry Bergman, Chester Conklin, Stanley Sandford, Hank Mann, Louis Natheax, Allen Garcia, Lloyd Ingraham, Wilfrid Lucas, Heine Conklin, Edward Kimball, John Rand and Charlie Chaplin.
>
> Music composed by Charles Chaplin.

The early part of the film is packed with comedy embracing all those forms customarily used by Chaplin. The old custard-pie technique has itself been mechanized, translated into terms of a feeding machine destined to speed up production by feeding the workers without loss of time. The feeding machine runs amok, and once more Charlie is victim to the malignant life of objects, as the machine pelts him with food, nuts and bolts, spills soup over him, rotates sweet corn furiously, and generally abuses him. Another superb episode is the one in which Charlie, a waiter now, replaces an absent "cabaret turn" and delivers himself of a gibberish song so amazingly presented that we understand every word where no words have been sung, a scene fit to rank with the David and Goliath sermon of *The Pilgrim* or the dance of the rolls in *The Gold Rush*.

Charlie has a nervous breakdown, and cannot stop the mechanical gesture with which he tightens bolts all day long; and then occur the unforgettable scenes in which this human machine runs amok and tightens everything remotely resembling a bolt—even to the buttons on a woman's, dress. Society then rejects the intractable and Charlie, leaving hospital, becomes one of the army of unemployed, and is responsible for one of the most brilliant ironies of the film.

Rushing to pick up a danger flag that has fallen from a lorry, he finds himself suddenly leading a parade of strikers, by virtue of having a red flag in his hands. Restored to liberty and poverty after a spell in prison as a political agitator, Charlie comes across another waif, a young girl. Every effort they make jointly to realize their dream of a little house, and a little garden and a little job ends in a journey in the Black Maria, until in the end they go off jauntily towards the horizon, towards the unknown, just as Charlie had done so many times alone.

1940—*The Great Dictator* (126 minutes). Released 15th October.

Cast: Charlie Chaplin, Jack Oakie, Henry Daniell, Billy Gilbert, Grace Hayle, Carter de Haven, Paulette Goddard, Maurice Moscovitch, Emma Dunn, Bernard Gorcey, Paul Weigel, Chester Conklin, Eddie Gribbon, Hank Mann, Leo White, Lucien Prival, Esther Michelson, Florence Wright, Robert O. Davis, Eddie Dunn, Peter Lynn and Nita Pike.

From the moment of Hynkel's first appearance, decked out with the glorious sign of the Double Cross, haranguing the mob with such hysterical violence that the very microphones bend back beneath its onslaught, in a glorious jabberwocky from which the superbly coined shtunk! emerges as Hynkel's key word, we have the perfect satirical presentation of Hitler and of all dictators. The very quality and cadences of voice are there, the phoney withdrawal to the consolation of music and solitude, the maniacal rages, the hypocritical fondling of babies, the monstrous bombast and theatrical effulgence of the mouse that tried to become a mountain. Parallel with this beautifully finished study, goes the debunking of Hitler and all he represented, beginning with the double-cross and ending with his replacement by the little Jewish barber.

Only Chaplin could bring forth belly laughs from such a subject at such a time. Witness the scene of the parley between the two dictators over their projected invasion of Austerlich, which degenerates into the most wildly funny custard pie fling since Mack Sennett days; or the glorious confusion arising out of Napoloni's arrival on an Imperial train that draws up in the wrong place; or the scene in which the two dictators, in barber's chairs, each strive to gain a vantage point from which they can look down on the other; or the superb scene filled with an irony light and delicate as a bubble, in which Hynkel juggles with a terrestrial globe, dancing with the world to the music of Lohengrin until the juggling becomes a ballet, until Hynkel caresses the globe with such energy and ardour that it bursts in his face, and he breaks down into hysterical sobbing.

The sentimentality of the film and its pathos are expressed in terms of the little Jewish barber—also played by Chaplin—and Hannah the Jewish refugee he befriends.

At the end of the film comes the famous harangue, delivered by Chaplin: (see Appendix B.)

1947—*Monsieur Verdoux* (125 minutes). Released 11th April.

Cast: Charlie Chaplin, Mady Correll, Allison Roddan, Robert Lewis, Audrey Betz, Martha Raye, Ada-May, Isobel Elsom, Marjorie Bennett, Helen Heigh, Margaret Hoffman, Marilyn Nash, Irving Bacon, Edwin Mills, Virginia Brissac, Almira Sessions, Eula Morgan, Bernard J. Nedell, Charles Evans, William Frawley, Barbara Slater, Christine Ell.

However fundamental and tragic the social implications of this film, there is great comedy in it, and the wonderful touches from a master hand, as when he starts laying breakfast for two, suddenly remembers the successful activities of the night, and methodically lays for one only; or the scene in which his beautifully expressive hands hover delicately, lovingly, over his roses, while in the background dense black smoke pouring from an incinerator marks the passing of a victim. His juggling with a tea cup, his backward fall through a window; above all, his magnificent scenes with Martha Raye, who has recorded her delight at working with so perfect a partner, are Chaplin at his comic best. Throughout, there is perfection of movement and gesture and mime, the subtlety of his most finished art in his most finished rôle.

1952—*Limelight* (150 minutes). Released 16th October.

    Cast: Charlie Chaplin, Claire Bloom, Sydney Chaplin, Nigel Bruce, Norman Lloyd, Buster Keaton, Marjorie Bennet, Andre Eglevsky, Melissa Hayden, Charles Chaplin, Jr., Wheeler Dryden. Chaplin produced, directed, starred, wrote the story and the screenplay, composed the music, including the words and music of three excellent music-hall songs, "The Sardine Song," "The Animal Trainer," and "Spring is Here," and a ballet entitled *The Death of Columbine*. He spent three years on the scenario and nine months on the score. The result is a haunting, nostalgic film filled with the warm, corny atmosphere of the old music halls. It is a film of contrasts—age and youth, failure and success, the young dancer at the beginning of her career and the clown at the end of his. It is illumined throughout by Chaplin's great gift of blending laughter with tears, as in the performance of the failing comedian, where everything is mis-timed, misdirected, and unendurably embarrassing as the voice becomes more jocular and more strained and agonized eyes look out of the sprightly clown's mask. There is the superb mime—of a rose, a stone, a Japanese tree: the ringmaster showmanship with all its great panache and the crack of a masterly whip given to a flea circus: and finally the excruciatingly funny act with Buster Keaton, on which moment of high comedy the great clown most fittingly dies. This is Chaplin's most personal film to date, and one fit to be placed among his greatest, in spite of some moments of banality. It is interesting to note that both his sons by Lita Grey are in the film; and three of his young children by Oona O'Neill—Geraldine, Michael and Josephine—make a brief appearance.

1957—A *King in New York* (105 minutes). Released Summer.

    Cast: Charlie Chaplin, Dawn Addams, Oliver Johnston, Maxine Audley, Harry Green, Phil Brown, John McLaren, Allan Gifford, Shani Wallis, Joy Nichols, Michael Chaplin, Joan Ingram, Sidney James, George Woodbridge, Jerry Desmonde, Robert Arden, Lauri Lupino-Lane, George Truzzi.

This is a satire on the American way of life which only partly comes off, perhaps because Chaplin was not yet able to reach the proper distance from his own involvement with it. Chaplin clearly enjoys his role as a deposed and penniless king who goes into television in order to maintain himself in the manner to which he has always, until now, been accustomed. He takes in a young waif, and so brings back far distant memories of *The Kid*, now lifted into quite another social class. There are moments we recognize—the sudden satire of modern cinema, the bathroom snoopers, the face-lift that comes undone when

A King in New York (1957)

A King in New York (1957)

the king in a nightclub laughs too much at the antics of two comedians. But the film, though it has flashes, is not among his best: and maybe Chaplin misses Charlie as much as we did. It will be interesting to see how he fills this great gap in future films.

APPENDIX B

✑ Some Writings of Charles Chaplin

1. *CHAPLIN ON THE SYMBOLISM OF HIS COSTUME.*

His little moustache? That is a symbol of vanity. His skimpy coat, his trousers so ridiculously baggy and shapeless? They are the caricature of our eccentricity, our stupidities, our clumsiness. *(This is obviously the reflective working out of an earlier subconscious inspiration, but the idea that the costume itself was a satire on humanity was probably with him from the beginning. So too the importance of the world-famous cane.)* The idea of the walking-stick was perhaps my happiest inspiration, for the cane was what made me speedily known. Moreover, I developed business with it to such a point that it took on a comic character of its own. Often, I found it hooked round someone's leg, or catching him by the shoulder, and in these ways I got a laugh from the public while I was myself scarcely aware of the gesture. I don't think I had fully understood in the beginning how much, among millions of individuals, a walking stick puts a label marked 'dandy' on a man. So that when I waddled on to the stage with my little walking stick and a serious air, I gave the impression of an attempt at dignity, which was exactly my aim.

2. *FROM* MY WONDERFUL VISIT (1922).

A description of the old blind man who was a familiar figure of his childhood, standing always under the bridge of Westminster Road: —

There he is, the same old figure, the same old blind man I used to see as a child of five, with the same old earmuffs, with his back against the wall and the same stream of greasy water trickling down the stone behind his back. The same old clothes, a bit greener with age, and the irregular bush of whiskers, coloured almost in a rainbow array, but with a dirty grey predominant. He has that same stark look in his eyes that used to make me sick as a child. Everything exactly the same, only a bit more dilapidated. . . . To me it is all too horrible. He is the personification of poverty at its worst, sunk in that inertia that comes of lost hope. It is too terrible.

The Children of Lambeth

As I pass, they look up. Frankly and without embarrassment, they look at the stranger with their beautiful kindly eyes. They smile at me. I smile back. Oh! if only I could do something for them. These waifs with scarcely any chance at all.

Kennington Park

How depressing to me are all parks! The loneliness of them. One never goes to a park unless one is lonesome. And lonesomeness is sad. The symbol of sadness, that's a park.

But I am fascinated now with it. I am lonesome, and want to be. Kennington Gate. That has its memories. Sad, sweet, rapidly recurring memories.

'Twas here my first appointment with Hetty. How I was dolled up in my little tight-fitting frock coat, hat and cane! I was quite the dude as I watched every street car until four o'clock, waiting for Hetty to step off, smiling as she saw me waiting.

I get out and stand there for a few moments at Kennington Gate. My taxi driver thinks I am mad. But I am forgetting taxi drivers. I am seeing a lad of nineteen, dressed to the pink, with fluttering heart, waiting, waiting for the moment of the day when he and happiness walked along the road. The road is so alluring now. It beckons for another walk, and as I hear a street car approaching I turn eagerly, for a moment almost expecting to see the same trim Hetty step off, smiling.

The car stops. A couple of men get out. An old woman. Some children. But no Hetty.

Hetty is gone. So is the lad with the frock coat and cane.

Kennington Cross

It was here that I discovered music, or where I first learned its rare beauty, a beauty that has gladdened and haunted me from that moment. It all happened one night when I was there. I recall the whole thing so distinctly.

I was just a boy, and its beauty was like some sweet mystery. I did not understand. I only knew I loved it and I became reverent as the sounds carried themselves through my brain via my heart.

Back of the Strand Theatre

He takes me to the back of the Strand Theatre, where there are beautiful gardens and courts suggesting palaces and armour and the days when knights were bold. These houses were the homes of private people during the reign of King Charles and even farther back. They abound in secret passages and tunnels leading up to the royal palace. There is an air about them that is aped and copied, but it is not hard to distinguish the real from the imitation. History is written on every stone; not the history of the battlefield that is laid bare for the historians, but that more intimate history, that of the drawing room, where, after all, the real ashes of empire are sifted.

The Old Tomato Man

I can picture him as he first appeared to me standing beside his round cart heaped with tomatoes, his greasy clothes shiny in their unkemptness, the rather glassy single eye that had looked from one side of his face staring at nothing in particular, but giving you the feeling that it was seeing all, the bottled nose with the network of veins spelling dissipation. I remember how I used to stand around and wait for him to shout his wares. His method never varied. There was a sudden twitching convulsion, and he leaned to one side, trying to straighten out the other as he did so, and then, taking into his one good lung all the air it would stand, he would let forth a clattering, gargling, asthmatic high-pitched wheeze, a series of sounds which defied interpretation.

And he was still there. Through summer suns and winter snows he had stood and was standing. Only a bit more decrepit, a bit older, more dyspeptic, his clothes greasier, his shoulder rounder, his one eye rather filmy and not so all-seeing as it once was. And I waited. But he did not shout his wares any more. Even the good lung was failing. He just stood there inert in his ageing. And somehow the tomatoes did not look so good as they once were.

Cami and Charlot

He is coming to me and we are both smiling broadly as we open our arms to each other.

"Cami!"

"Charlot!"

Our greeting is most effusive. And then something goes wrong. He is talking in French with the rapidity of a machine-gun. I can feel my smile fading into blankness. Then I get an inspiration. I start talking in English just as rapidly. Then we both talk at once. It's the old story of the irresistible force and the immovable body. We get nowhere.

Then I try talking slowly, extremely slowly.

"Do—you—understand?"

It means nothing. We both realize at the same time what a hopeless thing our interview is. We are sad a bit, then we smile at the absurdity of it.

He is still Cami and I am still Charlot, so we grin and have a good time anyhow.

Skaya

The song itself is plaintive, elemental, with the insinuating nuances that are vital to Russian music.

There comes a bit of melancholy in the song, and she sings it as one possessed, giving it drama, pathos. Suddenly there is a change. The music leaps to wild abandon. She is with it. She tosses her head like a wild Hungarian gypsy, and gives fire to every note. But almost as it began, the abandon is over. With wistful sweetness she is singing plaintively again.

She is touching every human emotion in her song. At times she is tossing away care, then gently wooing, an elusive strain that is almost fairylike, that crescendos into tragedy, going into crashing climax that diminishes into an ending, searching, yearning, and wistfully sad.

Her personality is written into every mood of the song. She is at once fine, courageous, pathetic and wild.

3. RHYTHM. *A Story of Men in macabre Movement*

CHARLES CHAPLIN

Only the dawn moved in the stillness of that small prison yard—the dawn ushering in death, as the young Loyalist stood facing the firing squad. The preliminaries were over. The small group of officials had stepped to one side to witness the end and now the scene had tightened into ominous silence.

Up to the last, the Rebels had hoped that a reprieve would come from Headquarters, for although the condemned man was an enemy to their cause, in the past he had been a popular figure in Spain, a brilliant writer of humour, who had contributed much to the enjoyment of his fellow countrymen.

The officer in charge of the firing squad knew him personally. Before the civil war they had been friends. Together they had been graduated from the university in Madrid. Together they had worked for the overthrow of the monarchy and the power of the Church. And together, they had caroused, had sat at nights around café tables, had laughed and joked, had enjoyed evenings of metaphysical discussion. At times they had argued on the dialectics of government. Their technical differences were friendly then, but now those differences had

From SCRIPT 15th January, 1938. Vol. xviii. No. 445.
Edited in Hollywood by Rob Wagner.
(The magazine has long since ceased to exist)
Information and copy of original by courtesy of Maurice Bessy, Director of the *Consortium de la Presse Cinèmatographique, Paris.* and part author*
of the recently published *Monsieur Chaplin ou Le Rire dans la Nuit.*
* With Robert Florey.

wrought misery and upheaval all over Spain, and had brought his friend to die by the firing squad.

But why think of the past? Why reason? Since the civil war, what good was reason? In the silence of the prison yard these interrogative thoughts ran feverishly through the officer's mind.

No. He must shut out the past. Only the future mattered. The future? A world in which he would be deprived of many old friends.

That morning was the first time they had met since the war. But never a word was spoken. Only a faint smile of recognition passed between them as they prepared for the march into the prison yard.

From the sombre dawn streaks of silver and red peered over the prison wall, and breathed a quiet requiem in rhythm with the stillness in the yard, a rhythm pulsating in silence like the throbbing of a heart. Out of that silence the voice of the commanding officer resounded against the prison walls. "Attention!"

At this command, six subordinates snapped their rifles to their sides and stiffened. The unity of their action was followed by a pause in which the next command was to be given.

But in that pause something happened, something that broke the line of rhythm. The condemned man coughed and cleared his throat. This interruption broke the concatenation of procedure.

The officer turned, expecting the prisoner to speak, but no words came. Turning to his men again, he was about to proceed with the next command, but a sudden revolt took possession of his brain, a psychic amnesia that left his mind a blank. He stood bewildered before his men. What was the matter? The scene in the prison yard had no meaning. He saw only objectively—a man with his back to the wall facing six others. And the group there on the side, how foolish they looked, like rows of clocks that had suddenly stopped ticking. No one moved. Nothing made sense. Something was wrong. It must all be a dream, and he must snap out of it.

Dimly his memory began to return. How long had he been standing there? What had happened? Ah, yes! He had issued an order. But what order came next?

Following "Attention!" was the command "present arms" and after that, "to aim", and then "fire!" A faint concept of this was in the back of his mind. But words to utter it seemed far off—vague and outside of himself.

In this dilemma he shouted incoherently, jumbled words that had no meaning. But to his relief the men presented arms. The rhythm of their action set his brain in rhythm, and again he shouted. Now the men took aim.

But in the pause that followed, there came into the prison yard hurrying footsteps, the nature of which the officer knew meant a reprieve. Instantly, his mind cleared. "Stop!" he screamed frantically at the firing squad.

Six men stood poised with rifles. Six men were caught in rhythm. Six men when they heard the scream to stop—fired.

4. *THE FINAL SPEECH IN* THE GREAT DICTATOR:
LET US UNITE

"I'm sorry, but I don't want to be an Emperor—that's not my business. I don't want to rule or to conquer anyone. I should like to help everyone, if possible—Jew and Gentile, Black, White.

We should all want to help one another; human beings are like that. We want to live by each other's happiness, not by each other's misery. We don't want to hate and despise one another. In this world there is room for everyone, and the good earth is rich, and can provide for everyone. The way of life could be free and beautiful.

But we have lost the way. Greed has poisoned men's souls; has barricaded the world with hate. It has goose-stepped us into misery and bloodshed. We have developed speed, but have shut ourselves in. Machinery that gives abundance has left us in want. Our knowledge has made us cynical. Our cleverness, hard and unkind. We think too much, and feel too little. More than machinery we need humanity. More than cleverness we need kindness and gentleness. Without these qualities life would be violent, and all would be lost.

The aeroplane and the radio have brought us closer together. The very nature of these inventions cries out for the goodness in man, cries out for universal brotherhood, for the unity of us all. Even now, my voice is reaching millions throughout the world—millions of despairing men, women and little children, victims of the system that makes men torture and imprison innocent people.

To those that can hear me I say, do not despair. The misery that is upon us is but the passing of greed, the bitterness of men who fear the way of human progress.

Hate of man will pass, and dictators die, and the power they took from the people will return to the people. And so long as men die, liberty will never perish.

Soldiers, don't give yourselves to brutes, men who despise you and enslave you, regiment your lives, tell you what to do, what to think and what to feel, who drill you, diet you, treat you like cattle, use you as cannon fodder. Don't give yourselves to these unnatural men— machine men with machine minds and machine hearts. You are not machines. You are not cattle. You are men. You have the love of humanity in your hearts, you don't hate. Only the unloved hate—the unloved and the unnatural.

Soldiers, don't fight for slavery, fight for liberty. In the 17th chapter of St. Luke it is written: 'The Kingdom of God is within man' —not one man, nor a group of men, but in all men. You the people have the power, the power to create machines, the power to create happiness. You people have the power to make this life free and beautiful, to make this life a wonderful adventure.

Then in the name of democracy, let us use that power. Let us all unite. Let us fight for a new world, a decent world that will give men a chance to work, that will give youth a future and old age a security.

By the promise of these things brutes have risen to power. But they lied. They do not fulfil that promise—they never will. Dictators free themselves, but they enslave the people.

Now, let us fight to fulfil that promise. Let us fight to free the world, to do away with national barriers, to do away with greed, with hate and intolerance. Let us fight for a world of reason—a world where science and progress will lead to all men's happiness. Soldiers, in the name of democracy, let us unite."

APPENDIX C

✎ The Little Fellow's Self-Portrait

(A review by Peter Cotes of Chaplin's *My Autobiography*. From *Films and Filming*, December, 1964.)

Charlie Chaplin has been called many splendid and shocking things in his time. "Charlie" by most of the world, "Charlot" by the French, "Chaplin" by many Americans—and a few other things as well—"The Tramp" by his interviewed self in print and, of course, "The Little Fellow" by his recorded self on film. (When *The Gold Rush* had a narration added in 1942, and Chaplin spoke his own description of his hero of that epic film, it was always "The Little Fellow" to whom he referred.)

From the sublime to the ridiculous we have been treated to thoughts from the great, near great, not so great, and those greatly ignorant, as to the precise greatness of this man as an artist. As though it is ever possible to define precisely that word "genius." That is why, although I like Sam Goldwyn's "He is the greatest artist we ever had" (which is a nice simple if somewhat bare tribute) only a little less than that startling statement of the noted historian, Emil Ludwig some years ago: "What is the fame of Gandhi compared with him who has shaken the world as only the figure of Christ has done before him? There is no one yet who has sustained such world-wide fame and yet remained so simple and unaffected", I still think that Bernard Shaw was nearer the mark than most when, after hailing Chaplin as "the only genius developed in motion pictures" he refused to embellish the description further and merely added "good wine needs no bush".

It is perhaps natural that with the word genius used so frequently about the Artist, not only in the past concerning his work but in the present as well, with the recent publication of his life, a reaction against such lavish praise would appear to have set in, and the press reviewers number those like Tynan (*Observer*) and Allsop (*Mail*) who failed to detect the artist and poet, as well as the superb comedian, in the pages of *My Autobiography by Charles Chaplin* (Simon & Schuster). They might both find time, however, to read the first third of the book again before committing themselves to the proposition that Chaplin can't write. Fortunately Rotha, Pritchett, Mortimer and Foot, as well as Katherine Whitehorn and Walter Allen on the BBC Critics programme saw the wood for the trees in what they produced to mark such a very important occasion, although on radio and even in TV'S

Panorama little was captured of Charlie's grandeur, the miracle of his total mastery in films. As Michael Foot said, "The marvel is not how little but how much of the real mind of genius he has succeeded in carrying from the screen to the printed page". But some are concerned only with just a few minimum moments from early shorts—and never the best moments—an insistence on his slum origins, drunken father, mad mother, and never a word about his tremendous emergence from all these handicaps.

In the millions of words written—constructive, destructive, loving, hating, admiring and denigrating about Chaplin the writer, because so many of the "panners" could not find it possible to assess just what this artist had got that Einstein, Wells and Shaw had all acclaimed as genius, few were as profound as Colin Hurry. In his *Premature Epitaphs* a few years back, he drew a picture—an example of the poet's lighter muse at its best—which caught Our Hero (who defies description as a writer every bit as much as he defies explaining as an artist) more successfully than the many weighty and lengthy assessments delivered to date, both about the actor and the producer-director-composer-scenarist, followed by the lover, controversial "politician" and now the writer :

> He'll catch St. Peter unawares
> Before the trumpet's blown
> He'll tumble up the golden stairs
> And trip before the throne
> He'll greet the cherubim with chaff
> And when the skies are riven
> With echoes of their cosmic laugh
> His sins will be forgiven.

Thus Colin Hurry on Charlie Chaplin. And whatever the "sins" committed by Mr. Chaplin in the writing of this book—well, may they be forgiven too; if only because of the enormous pleasure this work as a whole will afford to countless readers everywhere. For in the same way that Charlie acts with his body—"With all his body, limbs and torso" once wrote Eric Bentley—so Chaplin writes with a pen containing his heart. It was once said of the late Sean O'Casey, and well said, that the great Irish dramatist wrote with his heart's blood; Chaplin the writer also dips his pen in blood and writes from a heart, say some scoffers, which bears a remarkable likeness to a performance of an opera by Puccini played by a cheap touring company of little talent playing to empty houses; nevertheless this performance in a new sphere has warmth, nostalgia and, for me, truth. Nobody could have "ghosted" the first third of this book, and all of it—yes, even these references to other "greats" by the Great Man himself—represents to me a picture of the Kid looking at the other big fellows and actually being in awe of the celebrities with whom he has hobnobbed. This could be in others a rather tiresome name-dropping process to which we have become accustomed all too frequently in innumerable other "lives". But with Chaplin, like so much else with Charlie, the motive seems, to me at any rate, naïve, ingenuous and refreshing. Those five hundred pages alone could only have been written by the man who wrote the commentary for *The Gold Rush*, the music for the revised *Modern Times* when it was revived like the earlier masterpiece with a sound accompaniment several years ago, and the dialogue for *Lime-light*.

Ever generous with his almighty talent, in *My Autobiography* we are not doled out the record of a few years but the span of Chaplin's entire life to date. This volume, in excess of over 500 pages, would be worth its price if only for the first third alone, which beautifully por-trays his early life in and around Kennington, the English music-hall-setting at the turn of the century, and skilfully cuts from the sublime to the ridiculous, which so distinguishes his best work. He has an evoca-tive way of writing: a wonderful gift of creating the essence and atmosphere of a place and an epoch, or a mood or a transient moment. He had it all those years ago when he wrote about his visit to London, and he has it still. I was deeply moved, the more so, because he seems to be stating so simply and without any self-pity such a terrifying, stark and lonely childhood. Remembering the years of scurrilous "gutter" press campaigns he endured, I think a man like Chaplin, whose early years could have made him totally warped and abnormal but who was saved by his great gifts, who went first through the jungle of childhood poverty, then through the Hollywood cesspool, then became the most hated and hunted man in America, could well be excused for having, if he has, a few "dark patches" here and there in his mind and in his character.

Genius does not obey the ordinary rules of the game: and this genius had it hard. His father, whom he hardly ever saw save for a short period when he was living with him and his mistress, was a music-hall performer, a baritone who loved his bottle better than his family— mostly it was Charlie, his half-brother Syd, and his soubrette mother (stage name Lily Hartley) against the world, and what a remarkable trio they were! How improbable, and yet how revealing is his mother. Her theatrical career came to an end on the night when little Charlie, then barely five, made his first professional appearance as her under-study-cum-deputy after she had been booed off the stage by the troops at a canteen entertainment. In the pitilessness of youth, her little nipper gave a parody of his mother's voice cracking. Ironically enough, this brought the house down and earned the kid a shower of coppers from the audience. Thereafter she took spasmodically to nursing and needlework in a desperate attempt to keep her children off the streets. But all her efforts, the odd-jobbing of the wee toddlers and the sporadic financial assistance of her husband failed to keep them solvent. In an agony of despair, relieved by farce and family devotion, they drifted from lodging house to lodging house, each seedier than the last. Once they were transported like the Tramp in *City Lights* to luxurious living with a friend, but like that tragi-comedy episode, this too was short-lived. Eventually they finished up in the same Lambeth work-house where Louise, their father's mistress, was later to die.

Charlie and Sydney were soon sent to an orphanage and there followed the cycle of pathetic, hilarious and moving separations and reunions: Sydney in and out of the Merchant Navy, Charlie in and out of orphanages, Lily in and out of the work-house and then in and out of asylums. Happily, she lived long enough to see her two sons successful—one world-famous, enjoying the luxury and affluences she was never able to give them. However, she did give Charlie something more useful than anything else, something intangible but enduring enough for him to hold on to during those years of bitterness and grinding poverty; an infectious gaiety, an ability to laugh at the world and even at himself, and above all, the "prototype" of all his heroines. Down the years in his leading ladies—Edna, Georgia, Virginia, Paulette, Myrna and Marilyn—he managed to create a common image akin to the beauty and elusiveness of his mother, unashamedly sentimental, but defying serious criticism. Often, particularly in *The Gold Rush*, these "heroines" reflect also his love-hate relationship with his father's mistress.

Bitter as this life was, indeed annihilating to anyone of less resilience, in the end these early experiences proved invaluable. Where else could *The Tramp* have sprung from if not from the smiles and tears, pubs and cafes, music-halls and doss-houses of his childhood? Indeed, during his days with the Eight Lancashire Lads, Charlie and a fellow-performer, Bristol, invented an act called The Millionaire Tramps. Many incidental characters which crop up unexpectedly, yet with such a firm touch, throughout the films, seem equally to spring from those never-to-be-forgotten years. To name but one, Marceline, the great clown who fell on evil times and finally committed suicide, surely inspired "Calvero" in *Limelight* every bit as much as did the late Frank Tinney. His description of his boyhood "pash" for Mario Doro and their first meeting, could be the Little Fellow's first meeting with either Georgia in *The Gold Rush* or that flower-seller in *City Lights*. We meet incidents in his life over and over again which later we recognise as sequences used in his work, when as a great film star he looked back and remembered his music-hall boyhood. His memory served him well.

An aspect of Chaplin's early career is the enormous energy, industry and studying of his craft. True he went to no drama school, but from his mother's impersonations, personal observation of characters—he watched his father continually—and years of experience on the variety stage, he laid by an artistic banking account on which he was able to draw when the time was ripe. Contemporary "stars" who are with it today take note: glibly self-conscious technique and Top of the Pops fame which blossom overnight may wilt just as soon.

He draws the late John Barrymore with a few deft but damaging strokes, although for the most part there is no personal bitterness in the book. Indeed, he is warmly affectionate about many people, including his friend, that brilliant humorist Donald Ogden Stewart, who shared with him the tragic opening night disappointment over *Monsieur Verdoux* when that brilliant film was screened on Broadway at the height of the McCarthy heresy hunt just after Chaplin had been labelled *Public Enemy Number One* by Senator Joe's supporters.

Chaplin corrects by implication many mistakes in reference books and articles about himself. For example, the authoritative Encyclopaedia Britannica's statement that he appeared in the halls with both his father and his brother Sydney. It is significant also that he refers to the "Little Fellow" simply as The Tramp—perhaps his philosophy of life is sufficiently clear from his films, and we should not wish to pry further. But is it not a pity that we do not learn more about his artistic canons? The few pages we do get are so bright, tight and informative that we inevitably yearn for more. How apt is his dismissal of modern screen epics: "Superduper Specials". And I trust that some of our more pretentious and voluble exponents of The Method, who misconstrue Stanislavsky's teachings by a mumbling inaudibility and a roaming aimless ad-libbing about the stage, will read *this* Master's words on the craft of the actor: "The theory that one must know the character's life story is unnecessary. I abhor dramatic schools that indulge in reflections and introspections to evoke the right emotion. The mere fact that a student must be mentally operated upon is sufficient proof that he should give up acting".

Chaplin is equally blunt about some manifestations of kitchen-sink "realism" (sic) in the theatre, and likes the proscenium that separates the audience from the world of make-believe. He wants each scene to be revealed by the lifting of curtains, and dislikes plays that come over the footlights and participate with an audience, in which a character leans against the proscenium and explains the plot—"besides being didactic, this device destroys the charm of the theatre and is a prosaic way of getting over exposition". In a word, he prefers stage "magic" to the very untheatrical "method". Stanislavsky would have agreed.

My Autobiography is well produced and indexed, despite some notable omissions (e.g. Wee Georgie Wood, George Robey and Will Murray are but three whom I happen to know he knew well) and such shortcomings as odd mis-spellings (e.g. "Billie" for "Billy" the pageboy in *Sherlock Holmes* who Master Charles Chaplin portrayed well over a half-century ago at The Duke of York's Theatre). It is a "must" for all who value the film as an artistic medium and wish to pay homage to its greatest son. He who was, after all, a product of our English music-hall in its hey-day and at the height of all its blazing glory. But from which, too, "only he could develop that inimitable quality of motion, a blend of dance, drollery and poetic sensitivity that distinguishes his work from that of others" wrote Paul Rotha with rare perception when reviewing the volume under discussion and this aspect of Chaplin's work only the other day.

And just as reams have been written, and millions upon millions of words spoken during the last few weeks about Charlie Chaplin in all his many and varied states, both in the past and the present, so few will dispute his description of himself in this long-awaited self-portrait. Besides serving as a fitting close it also assesses his place in the hall of fame and unconsciously awards him the mantle of posterity: "Besides I was a pantomimist and in that medium I was unique and, without false modesty, a master".

I would go further; looking back over Chaplin's legendary career as actor, director, producer, musician and screen-writer, and his creation of Charlie, the world's greatest comedian, the best known figure of our day, and an art which ranged from the pinnacles of high comedy to the ocean depths of human despair, I would call him The First Artist of modern times.

✍ Bibliographical Note

THE FOLLOWING WORKS HAVE BEEN CONSULTED:

My Wonderful Visit. Charles Chaplin. Hurst & Blackett. 1922.
A Comedian Sees the World. Charles Chaplin.
Charlie. Louis Delluc (trans. Hamish Miles). Bodley Head Ltd. 1922.
Charlie Chaplin. His Life and Art. William D. Bowman. Routledge. 1931.
Chaplin, Last of the Clowns. Parker Tyler. Vanguard Press. 1948.
Charlot. Philippe Soupault. Plon. 1931.
Charlie Chaplin Intime. May Reeves (Souvenirs Recueillis par Claire Goll). N. R. F. Gallimard. 1935.
La Vérité sur Charlie Chaplin, sa vie, ses amours, ses déboires. Carlyle T. Robinson (Traduit et adapté par René Lelu). Paris. Société Parisienne d'Edition.
Charlot, ou la naissance d'un mythe. Pierre Leprohon. Corymbe. Paris. 1935.
Charles Chaplin. Pierre Leprohon. Jacques Melot. Paris. 1946.
Hollywood d'Hier et d'Aujourdhui. Robert Florey. Paris. 1948.
An Index to the Films of Charles Chaplin. Theodore Huff. Special Supplement to *Sight and Sound.* Index Series, No. 3. March, 1945.

Behind the Screen. Sam Goldwyn. Grant Richards. 1924.
Marie Tempest. Hector Bolitho. Cobden-Sanderson. 1936.
Circus Parade. John S. Clarke. Batsford. 1936.
Movies for the Millions. Gilbert Seldes. Batsford. 1937.
Remember Fred Karno. Edwin Adeler and Con West. Long. 1939.
Film. Roger Manvell. Pelican Books. 1946.
Histoire Générale du Cinéma. Vols. 1 and 2. Georges Sadoul. Paris. 1947.
The Art of the Film. Ernest Lindgren. Allen and Unwin. 1948.
A Writer's Notebook. W. Somerset Maugham. Heinemann. 1949.

ESSAYS IN:

Alarums and Excursions. James Agate. Grant Richards. 1922.
Cinema. C. A. Lejeune. Maclehose. 1931.
Assorted Articles. D. H. Lawrence. Secker. 1932.
While Rome Burns. Alexander Woolcott. Viking Press. 1934.
Garbo and the Night Watchmen. Alistair Cooke. Cape. 1937.
The Poisoned Crown. Hugh Kingsmill. Eyre and Spottiswoode. 1944.
Chestnuts in Her Lap. C. A. Lejeune. Phoenix House Ltd. 1947.
Horizon. Vol. 17. No. 19. March, 1948.

Penguin Film Review. No. 7 (1948), No. 9 (1949).
Sight and Sound. Spring, Summer, 1946; Summer, 1949.
Sequence. Spring, 1948; Spring, 1949.
Charlot. Le Disque Vert. Paris/Bruxelles. 1924.
Charlie Chaplin. Theodore Huff. 1952.
Monsieur Chaplin. M. Berry and R. Florey. 1952.

INDEX